# PRAISE FOR
# BETTER THAN MY DREAMS

"When the dream you thought your life would be gets shattered, it's hard to see the sovereignty of God among the broken pieces—let alone, the goodness of God. In *Better Than My Dreams* we see both. And something else. We see something beautiful. And that something beautiful is the dream God first dreamed of when He dreamed of you, and when He dreamed of me."

—Ken Gire
Author, *Windows of the Soul* and *Moments with the Savior*

"Whether you are wrestling with overwhelming challenges or just experiencing low-grade disillusionment in life (as we all do at times), Paula's out-of-the-box thinking will help you get God out of whatever box you may have Him in. Her wisdom and insight will open your eyes to the joy of truly *living* life—not the life we always dreamed of, but one that's even better—the one we already have!"

—Shannon Ethridge, MA
Best-selling Author, *Every Woman's Battle* and *Completely His*

"With remarkable insight, Paula Rinehart cuts to the chase, revealing the longings, disappointments, dreams, challenges, and spiritual hunger of every woman. If you long for a book that describes your deepest desires and leads you on a journey to joy, look no further. Paula's writing is fresh, vibrant, penetrating, and personal. The built-in study guide makes this book ideal for personal or small group study."

—Carol Kent
Speaker and Author, *A New Kind of Normal*

D1015166

"Desire is often an undeclared war in the heart. We want, and we don't get. We fail to receive because we either don't ask or we ask for what will divert us from glory. Desire is the territory where we battle with the core questions about the goodness and power of God. Paula Rinehart is a wise, generous, and honest woman who knows this terrain and has found in her own struggle a sweet passion for the risen, self-giving love of Jesus. Her invitation is so profound and yet so simple it is staggering: find the passion you were born to engage, and in giving you will find the deepest desire aroused and fulfilled beyond measure. *Better Than My Dreams* will transform and refine every heart that risks desiring God."

—Dan B. Allender, PhD
President and Professor of Counseling, Mars Hill
Graduate School; and Author, *The Wounded Heart*,
*To Be Told*, and *Leading with a Limp*

"From the first paragraphs I felt like Paula was reading my mind and my heart, and it was hard to put the book down. With a style that made me feel as though we were sitting in her office talking about life, she encouraged me to be honest about the disappointments in my life and to ask God to meet me there. It's a book of great encouragement and hope."

—Alison Pollock
Associate Campus Director, Campus Crusade for Christ

"*Better Than My Dreams* is a must-read for women of all ages and stages of life. Paula is gifted with a divine ability to help women recognize and deal with real-life issues, thereby enabling women to live beyond their wildest dreams. Practical applications and the small group guide are most helpful in our journey to live life to the fullest and make progress in our walk with the Lord."

—Debbie Stuart
Director, Women's Ministry, Prestonwood Baptist Church, Plano, TX

"Sooner or later every woman feels stuck in her own life. Thankfully, Paula Rinehart has been there and knows the way out . . . with honesty, compassion, and a steady vision for the life we women long for."

—Carla Barnhill
Author, *The Myth of the Perfect Mother*

"Come, all you who are weary and wounded, and find hope. 'Disappointment is, strangely enough,' Rinehart writes, 'the doorway to real adventure with God.' How thankful I am for such an articulate Christian woman, using the truths of Scripture to set us free. Life is *so* hard, yet that pain can be 'a gymnasium for the soul.' I was compelled by *Better Than My Dreams*, turning pages to the satisfying end."

—Dee Brestin
Author, *The Friendships of Women, Falling in Love with Jesus,* and *A Woman of Worship*

"Insightful, honest, and beautifully eloquent, Paula Rinehart gives a voice to what all of us women already know—we have big dreams for ourselves. Regardless of our seasons in life, our longing to find deeper meaning unites us. Written with transforming truth, *Better Than My Dreams* is a book for every woman everywhere. It is a practical and hands-on approach to our quest for more. I will wholeheartedly share it with all of my friends!"

—Lisa Whittle
Speaker and Author, *The Seven Hardest Things God Asks a Woman to Do* and *Behind Those Eyes*

"Rinehart's book reads like a velvet plow, gently but relentlessly breaking up the frozen tundra of our souls, making way for a radiant hope. With the turn of each page, the alluring possibility of a life—with its losses and longings included—drenched with God's irrepressible goodness begins to glow. Rinehart's book is a wise and beautiful offering, one worth a profoundly warm reception."

—Connally Gilliam
Navigator Metro Mission Staff, Washington, DC; and Author,
*Revelations of a Single Woman*

"Paula's book points at the elephant in the room—our mistaken belief that our faith will somehow fix every heartache we face. But more than pointing out the elephant, she points us to the God who is far grander and far sweeter than a life lived as a fairy tale. Thank you, Paula, for the bracing freedom of reality and the reminder of a love that never lets us go."

—Sally Breedlove
Board Member, Anglican Mission in America; and Author, *Choosing Rest*

"The secret . . . the secret to life. How much would that be worth to you? Paula Rinehart pulls back the curtain, exposing secrets to living the life of Jesus that I certainly wish someone had given me years ago. If you are wanting to live the life Christ intended for you, amidst this confusing, messy, broken world, this book is for you. Paula takes well-known truths of Scripture and brings them near where they can be experienced and their implications embraced. She has a wonderful way of walking amidst the reality of most of our not-so-perfect lives and the ravenous hunger we have been gifted with by God for so much more. Paula doesn't offer an easy path, but she offers motivating and deeply practical ways to taste more of all God has for those He has chosen and calls His beloved. This book will help you live the life God longs for you to enjoy. If it were up to me, I would make it mandatory reading in the Life 101 course!"

—Dr. Cheryl L. Meredith, PhD
Vice President, Missions/Human Resources, The Navigators

"As I read *Better Than My Dreams*, I was shaken to the depths of my heart as I was faced with the reality of my own belief in who God truly is. I was challenged to see my life and how God views me. I have repeatedly asked God to take away some problem, trial, or difficulty in my life, and sometimes He has. But this book has helped me to ask a new question when God does not remove the problem, and that is 'Will I let God transform me in this?' Those who read this book will be convicted, challenged, encouraged, and ready for God's transformation."

—Alana Combs
Women's Mentor

"All of us who have watched Disney's *Cinderella* know the first line of that famous song. 'A dream is a wish your heart makes when it's fast asleep.' Some go through life fast asleep, still holding on to their dreams. But what do you do when you wake up and realize that your dreams are not there? Paula Rinehart's new book *Better Than My Dreams* gives you gentle reality and a tender hope in a world of broken dreams. She warmly takes you by your delicate heart and walks you through the charred brokenness, then kindly helps you see that every shattered dream is never wasted in the hands of our loving heavenly Father. I believe as you read her book, you will discover for yourself how precious your broken dreams are to Him and how He longs to use them in your life just for you. I encourage all women who have dreams that have never come true to embark on a personal journey with the living God through this book so you may find freedom on the other side of those dreams."

—Senior Master Sergeant Brenda West
162nd Arizona Air National Guard

"There were moments reading *Better Than My Dreams* when my breath caught to hear what seemed like my own voice breaking from Paula's pages. So deeply does this wise friend and mentor resonate with our own stories of shattered dreams that we feel known, accompanied, and encouraged to risk crossing our own scary yet holy thresholds. Doorways that lead not into what we most fear but improbably and wondrously into something we could not imagine . . . joy, freedom, and intimacy with the One who redeems all our broken pieces into the original masterpiece that we were always created to be."

—Susan New
Well Women Ministries

"Having lost my youngest daughter to a tragic car accident just three months ago, I believe Paula's book was sent to me by God at just the right time. It is full of encouragement for those suffering the disappointments of life and lost dreams. Her stories remind us that God walks with us and we don't have to rely on what worked in the past. To read this book is to feel freedom and anticipation as you let go of what you thought you needed and enter the journey as a 'dance with God' and the fulfillment of dreams."

—Cheryl Baker
Director, Women's Ministries and Leadership Development,
Perimeter Church, Atlanta, GA

# BETTER
## THAN MY
# DREAMS

# BETTER
## THAN MY
# DREAMS

*Finding What You Long For
Where You Might Not Think to Look*

## PAULA RINEHART

**THOMAS NELSON**
*Since 1798*

NASHVILLE   DALLAS   MEXICO CITY   RIO DE JANEIRO

Published in Nashville, Tennessee by Thomas Nelson. Thomas Nelson is a registered trademark of Thomas Nelson, Inc.

Published in association with Greg Johnson, WordServe Literary, 10152 Knoll Circle, Highlands Ranch, CO 80130, www.wordserveliterary.com.

Thomas Nelson, Inc. titles may be purchased in bulk for educational, business, fund-raising, or sales promotional use. For information, please e-mail SpecialMarkets@ThomasNelson.com.

Many of the names used in this book and the story details have been changed to protect the privacy of those individuals.

All Scripture quotations, unless otherwise indicated, are taken from The New American Standard Bible®, © 1960, 1962, 1963, 1968, 1971, 1972, 1973, 1975, 1977, 1995 by The Lockman Foundation. Used by permission.

Scripture quotations noted NIV are taken from the Holy Bible, New International Version®. © 1973, 1978, 1984 by International Bible Society. Used by permission of Zondervan Publishing House. All rights reserved.

Scripture quotations noted KJV are taken from the King James Version of the Bible. Public domain.

Scripture quotations marked NKJV are taken from The New King James Version®. © 1982 by Thomas Nelson, Inc. Used by permission. All rights reserved.

Scripture quotations noted MSG are taken from *The Message* by Eugene H. Peterson. © 1993, 1994, 1995, 1996, 2000, 2001, 2002. Used by permission of NavPress Publishing Group. All rights reserved.

**Library of Congress Cataloging-in-Publication Data**
Rinehart, Paula.
 Better than my dreams : finding what you long for where you might not think to look / Paula Rinehart.
  p. cm.
 Includes bibliographical references.
 ISBN 978-0-8499-1867-4 (pbk.)
 1. Christian women—Religious life. I. Title.
BV4527.R56 2007
248.8'43—dc22

2007012273

*Printed in the United States of America*
10 11 12 13 EPAC 8 7 6 5

*To every woman who's had a broken dream . . .*
*and lived to see the mercy beyond.*

# CONTENTS

# ACKNOWLEDGMENTS

*This book has been so many years in the forming that, honestly,* I could thank nearly everyone I know, beginning with my mother. That being said, there are a number of individuals whose faces come to mind.

I think especially of Karen D'Arezzo, Helen Crawford, and Jeri White—women whose early and sacrificial witness taught me not just to appreciate the Bible, but to love the Word of God as truth that is able to shape one's deepest life.

To my husband, Stacy, whose original and sacrificial encouragement in this shaky enterprise of writing has sustained me in many a bug-killing hour.

To Marnie Holden and Brent Curtis (author with John Eldredge of *The Sacred Romance*), my gratitude for the way God used your friendship to keep me grounded during a period of my life when I was more than a little disheartened.

To two wonderful children, Allison and Brady, now grown, I am grateful for your willingness to allow some of your own story to be told and to "suffer the effects" of having a mother who writes.

To Jennifer Ennis, I am indebted to twenty years of friendship and a thousand conversations God has used to shape so much of my own understanding about life.

To Debbie Wickwire of Thomas Nelson and Greg Johnson

of WordServe Literary for your confidence and hard work on this project.

I grow more grateful each year for C. S. Lewis, whom I never met but feel as though I have always known. His writings have been a steady companion to me over three decades.

My thanks to those who served with us in CoMission from 1990 to 1995 and who invested a year of their lives in the former Soviet Union, teaching about Christ in Russian public schools. I have included two stories from that era, born of the deep conviction that we must get outside our own culture to really appreciate what God is doing in our day.

To the congregation of Blacknall Memorial Presbyterian Church in Durham, North Carolina, my gratitude for the privilege of participating in the worship that occurs in your midst.

To a host of women I've met here and abroad who have taught me so much about how the gospel is fleshed out in our lives and who have graciously allowed their stories to be told in camouflage and for the building up of others.

Finally, I thank the Lord for the great joy of offering words in his name, for the touch of his mercy on my life, and for enabling this effort to be completed over a year such that no one could rightfully expect to write a book.

*Blessed are those whose strength is in you,*
*who have set their hearts on pilgrimage.*

—PSALM 84:5 NIV

# A RITE OF PASSAGE

# Chapter 1

# A DIFFERENT KIND OF WONDERFUL

## SOMETHING BETTER THAN THE LIFE YOU DREAMED OF

*Our rest is as far as the fire-drake swings*
*And our peace is put in impossible things.*
—G. K. CHESTERTON

*This I recall to my mind, therefore have I hope.*
*It is of the LORD's mercies that we are not consumed,*
*because his compassions fail not.*
*They are new every morning: great is thy faithfulness.*
—LAMENTATIONS 3:21-23 KJV

*In recent years I have begun to notice unexpected moments* where I feel a delicious stirring of hope. It's a wild and unusual feeling, as it often occurs in situations that, humanly speaking, look pretty bleak.

Let me explain a little more. As a counselor, I listen to women share their stories all day long. I hear about the real stuff of their lives, which is not unlike my own. And as I listen to stories of, say, a father's death or a mother's drinking problem or a spouse's neglect, I am discovering that no matter what the specific circumstances may be, truly, we are all telling the same story—of loves and hopes, of our failures and our fears.

Our stories are like patchwork quilts we stitch together during seasons of joy or duress into a kind of security blanket we carry through life.

As I listen to a woman talk about her quilt or as I consider my own, two words often come to mind. *But God.*

If, in trying to face our lives head-on, all we had in our hands were a few psychological tools and a smattering of the best human self-help, just how lost would we stay? How condemned would we be to an endless repeating of the same-old, same-old, stuck forever in a morass of (mostly) our own making?

But God.

> *Our stories are like patchwork quilts we stitch together during seasons of joy or duress into a kind of security blanket we carry through life.*

Perhaps this is why such a wild hope is stirred in me. For what I hear now, in other women's stories, is the first rumblings of something I've stumbled upon myself.

The struggle is a door, and inside God waits. If you are willing to walk through the portal, you find what you could not experience deeply any other way. The gospel comes to life there. The power to forgive yourself and everybody else . . . a crack at discovering the way God actually redeems what seems irredeemable . . . the hope of seeing him create a new ending out of a bad beginning—it's all waiting to be fleshed out.

There is really Someone there, in whose company lies the love you have longed for since you took your first breath.

## BY A STRANGE ROUTE

What also surprises me about this wild hope is that it's such a sharp contrast to what I've experienced in other seasons of my life. By my midthirties, I had become one of the more disillusioned Christians I've known, then or since. I worked hard to keep my skepticism quiet, as it felt distinctly like a virus that others might catch.

If someone had asked me what was wrong, though, I could have offered only a vague response. "I'm not sure . . . Life just isn't working out like I planned."

*But did you have a plan, exactly?*

"Well, no," I would have replied. "But God had a plan, didn't he? You know what they say: 'God loves you and has a wonderful plan for your life.'" And then I might have added under my breath that my present experience didn't qualify as anybody's standard definition of *wonderful*.

So, no, I didn't exactly have a plan . . . but I did have distinct pictures in my mind of how I thought my life would look. Through the hazy outlines of the future I saw everything with a golden glow—marriage to a man who could complete my unspoken thoughts and children who lined up their lives as neatly as their shoes. I wanted a vibrant ministry to women and a quiet, lovely house on a hill. And I thought God would offer some sort of immunity from anything that deeply disturbed this happy picture.

On some unconscious level, I projected my present into the future and squared the whole equation. When I first discovered Christ during my college years, I felt like a kid who'd joined the traveling circus—or like Lucy must have felt when she fell out the back of an old wardrobe into the sparkling daze of Narnia. I was amazed at the hope of actually shedding my old self and slowly *becoming* the person God had in mind before my parents thought to conceive me. To think that I could be forgiven—flat-out forgiven, with no questions asked. That I was given a place in a spiritual family with bonds deeper than culture or race or trust accounts. It was incredible. *It is incredible* . . . but in a different way than I understood then.

> *I didn't know I had stapled old dreams onto a new faith.*

I took my faith and projected it into the future in rather concrete terms. These pictures in our minds are images we don't even know are there—until the videos of our lives play out differently. That was the disillusionment of my thirties. I didn't know I had stapled old dreams onto a new faith. My dreams were a warm coat, firmly attached, and they got baptized right along with the rest of me. I had created a sort of unspoken pact with God—only he hadn't signed off on the deal.

Only slowly, I think, do we separate hope from illusion. Only with time can you see the outlines of the actual dream God is shaping in and through you. For what seemed like forever, I saw only that marriage and raising children and ministry and writing books—and nearly everything—had far more challenges than anticipated. Where was the golden glow?

This movement from expectations to disillusionment to a different sort of hope is a spiritual rite of passage, I've discovered. Hope is the golden stuff that draws us along on this journey. It keeps us alive on the inside so we can actually taste and experience the wonder of belonging to God. The richness of his mercy. A power to love that is not our own.

> *On some unconscious level, I projected my present into the future and squared the whole equation.*

Hope is a container God shapes in your heart where faith and love can be stored—and then generously offered to others.

The journey itself, though, is often not what we expect. It can be full of detours and potholes and narrow paths. Or perhaps I should say that God has a different sort of wonderful than the one we have in mind.

## WANTING THE GOOD DREAM

As you step out into life, the heat gets turned up on your dreams and desires and expectations. Your longings surface—as, indeed, they are meant to. Perhaps you didn't know you wanted a baby so much, for example, until you could not get pregnant. You might have felt the longing to be married more intensely, as good men seemed in short supply. Life has a way of awakening our hearts in big ways, and pain of some sort is usually the megaphone.

My daughter's experience is not unlike that of many, many women. The pain in her life was not the experience of infertility, but the anguish of repeated miscarriages. She would get pregnant, start to celebrate, and plan—and then the symptoms of losing a baby would begin. It was a miserable roller coaster to ride. Her friends were having babies like rabbits—babies, in some cases, they weren't even trying to have. And Allison had wanted a child since she was ten years old. She would trade her CPA for a diaper bag in a heartbeat.

*This movement from expectations to disillusionment to a different sort of hope is a spiritual rite of passage.*

Not being able to have a child threw my daughter on God like nothing else.

Many good things had come her way, easily enough, growing up. But a child—this was something that her accountant's soul could not account for and her engineer husband could not make happen. Her nose was pressed against the window of mystery—where some dreams miraculously come true and others never do.

After the grief of each miscarriage, I would offer her the

same feeble words of comfort, which grew less comforting each time. *You'll have a child, honey, when you aren't thinking so hard about it.* I would suggest a couple of diversions. *How about a pottery class, or French cooking?* But she only grew more desperate, and she had questions of her own.

"Mom," she wrangled, "why is God holding out on me? Why doesn't he do this simple thing?"

Allison was up against that special enigma a woman experiences when she knows she longs for something God himself has created her to desire. This is not an ache for a fur coat. What could be more right than wanting to be a mother? A good desire—the right desire—that still doesn't happen . . . now there is a challenge to explain.

In these conversations, I had less and less to say. I couldn't make the situation better, which is a hard place for any mother. And yet, by some fine irony, this was the very sort of mother-anguish my daughter wanted more than anything in the world.

How, indeed, do we explain these sorts of experiences? And who among us travels very far in life without running headlong into the gap between what we hoped for and what came to pass? Are there women out there who have never known the miscarriage of a good dream—one that really mattered in a big way?

> *Who among us travels very far in life without running headlong into the gap between what we hoped for and what came to pass?*

All thoughts to the contrary, God does not always provide a detour lane around a broken dream.

## THE WAY DREAMS MUTATE

So there are perfectly obvious disappointments that come our way. There's more than a bit of mystery surrounding the good dreams for which God says *no* or *wait*.

But dreams and expectations in life, especially in our culture, have a curious way of inflating. Simple hope can harden into expectation and even demand. We live in an atmosphere of demand, where a problem is something to be solved, not endured, and suffering is seen as an intruder. We are told over and over that our lives should be a certain way—and we each have our own notions of what that looks like.

> *Dreams and expectations in life, especially in our culture, have a curious way of inflating.*

A conversation with a good friend over coffee one day reminded me how easily this supersizing of expectation happens.

She was talking about a mutual acquaintance who seemed to have a rather enviable life with very few wrinkles. "But then," my friend explained, "she's always had 'the package.'"

"The package?" I asked. "What's 'the package'?"

"Oh, you know," she replied. "She went to the right school and married a sharp guy she met there. They moved into the established neighborhood his great job afforded. They have two little girls with bows in their hair, and she's working on her own career goals, a little at a time. They've got a supportive family and a wonderful church. That's the package."

*Oh, wow,* I thought. *I guess that is a package.* Of course, we know that things are rarely as good as they look and there's a worm in every apple. Still, I thought about what she said for days. It struck me how all of us—every generation, every kind of background—we all fashion images in our heads of the life we think would make us happy. Maybe it's not two little girls with bows in their hair—but trust me, it's something. And that vision easily calcifies into a package.

The irony is that this drift from hope . . . to expectation . . . to demand is a trap that is much easier to fall into as a Christian. C. S. Lewis was right: coming into a relationship with Jesus is, indeed, like falling out of the back of a wardrobe into the fresh wonder of a whole new world where anything can happen. Aren't we all acquainted with Jesus' words "with God

> *We all fashion images in our heads of the life we think would make us happy.*

all things are possible" (Matt. 19:26)? It's so easy to fill in the blank called "all things" with a script God never quite had in mind—or to assume that knowing Jesus will somehow spare you a heartache he actually intends to walk you through.

## ENTITLEMENT: WANTING LIFE
## ON OUR TERMS

When our sticky fingers get wrapped around our dreams—when hope has mutated into an agenda that God is supposed to fulfill—then we are living from a place of entitlement. That's a hard word, one I could scarcely recognize in my own life until I ran square into such stinging disappointments they felt like yellow jackets at a carefully laid-out picnic.

Traveling among Christians in other cultures has helped me see the inflated notions I've carried around most of my life. I stand amazed at the sheer joy of women in Romania who for years met in parked cars in the dead of winter to study their Bibles because there was no other welcome spot. I am humbled by the example of Chinese couples who get excited about my husband's leftover protein bars because they have no other food for the long train ride home. In the air I breathe, it's annoying to get stuck in traffic too long. And joy, unfortunately, is often reserved for pinnacle experiences—when it is meant to be the background music to my everyday life with God.

What I'm saying is that the virus of entitlement will eventually steal from you nearly everything that's good. It will bar the door to a genuine, honest experience with God that includes the best of times—and some of the worst—all in the same container.

Inflated expectations take you to an artificial place. They can work a real number on the way you see God. For when your life does not play out like the movie in your mind—when there's divorce or infertility, rejection or betrayal in your path—God may look more like Scrooge, withholding something you vitally need. He's let you down. He's left you by the side of the road to fend for yourself. That's the darker side of where we go when we cling to this invisible demand of entitlement.

*Joy, unfortunately, is often reserved for pinnacle experiences—when it is meant to be the background music to my everyday life with God.*

When I suspect the presence of this virus in my life, I am often drawn to a piercingly accurate comment made by a man of the faith many years ago. I've never forgotten his words. J. B. Phillips, one of the first translators of the New Testament into modern English, wrote this:

> The people who feel that God is a disappointment have not understood the terms on which we inhabit this planet.[1]

Phillips is saying that for true joy and hope to take hold of us, we have to begin from an altogether different place. We must understand the terms on which we inhabit this planet. This is a broken world, riddled with heartache, in desperate search of a Savior—not "a well-run kindergarten where good is rewarded and evil punished."[2]

I am not living in the land of neat packages.

The actual starting place—the terms on which we inhabit

the planet—is closer to the prophet Jeremiah's take on things. "It is of the LORD's mercies that we are not consumed," he said (Lam. 3:22 KJV). No sense of entitlement there! Nothing is a given, really, not even my next breath. We are not in a position to demand. It's all a gift. That's a very different orientation to life and to God, but it is true north. Follow that path and gratitude will not be far behind.

## LIFE AS A JOURNEY

So we encounter somewhere along the way this rite of passage, this *right-sizing* of expectation about life. You have probably discovered some of the same realities I have—that marriages and close relationships require a world of give and take, that your children have challenges even the best mother can't remedy. Perhaps you have been blindsided by a couple of stinging losses you didn't see coming—or felt like a character in a play who suddenly finds herself saying someone else's lines, as though you were reading from the wrong script and this experience could not be part of your life. But it is.

Hardly any of us travel very far without encountering at least one huge disappointment. One blot of black paint on an otherwise charming canvas. One obstacle in our path that simply refuses to yield. I used to think this was just my experience in life. And then I started to pay closer attention. No one comes through unscathed. And those who appear to do so are usually just better pretenders.

Life is uncertain. Coming to grips with that uncertainty,

in the deep places of your heart, is like breaking through a sound barrier—or waking up after a long, long nap. It's like a conversation I had with a woman trying to decide whether to marry a man she'd waited years to meet.

Her story was this. Her clearest memories of childhood were the hours she spent by the bed of her father as he died a slow, sad death from Lou Gehrig's disease. In her little-girl mind, she thought that with her presence and her help, he would get better. At least she could bring him a few moments of joy. And so she sat there dutifully—hour after hour, month after month until he died.

She had grown into a compassionate woman in her thirties, with a depth and gentleness that made her a superb nurse. And finally—finally—she'd met a man who felt worth the wait. She was all set to marry him. Only, in a particular twist of irony, this man was battling an illness as well. It wasn't life threatening, but it was chronic. And it was way too close to home for her.

Her heart wanted to move forward in the relationship, but her head searched for some

> *There are precious few guarantees about the things that matter most. God is the only certainty.*

assurance that she would not be sitting by another man's bedside down the road. "I want to know that I won't repeat that earlier pain," she admitted, understandably.

*I know you do,* I thought. Oh, for a few guarantees. I wished like crazy I could offer her some. But our conversations were more about <u>making peace with the terms of this planet</u>—that there are precious few guarantees about the things that matter most. <u>God is the only certainty.</u> So if my future holds some repeat of my past (which is sometimes the case), then what I know is that he will be there. <u>Jesus will still be there.</u> And my experience of his love and care in those moments is what will make for a new chapter and not an old bad dream. It's an incredible dance of trust.

Do you remember when you first really understood how fragile life is? Do you recall what was happening in your life when you realized that God did not promise some sort of immunity from pain—and he didn't provide a protective coating so you wouldn't actually feel it? That there aren't any guarantees? For each of us, life holds a few Humpty Dumpty experiences where it feels like all the king's horses and all the king's men couldn't put this thing together again. And God eventually takes those broken pieces and fashions something far better than anything we could even think to dream.

> *God eventually takes those broken pieces and fashions something far better than anything we could even think to dream.*

I want to suggest that it's just these places in your experience—where dreams and expectations don't work out—that you are being issued the invitation of your life. Disappointment is, strangely enough, a doorway to the real adventure. It's the point where you start to leave behind most of your notions of how your story should read—and enter your relationship with God as a journey. A true journey, one that's wild and adventurous and not anywhere close to predictable.

When I lived in Colorado Springs, years ago, I remember one of Brent Curtis's offhand comments, spoken in a casual moment of reflection before he wrote *The Sacred Romance*.[3]

"I feel like I am just beginning to know God," he said. And I thought, *That's a strange thing to say, Brent. You've been a Christian for years.*

I realize now that Brent was speaking of this thing of journey—a kind of emotional conversion that comes as you stop living on the edge of straining to get God to do what you have in mind. The freedom to actually be on an adventure with God becomes strangely possible when you aren't pushing so hard for The Package. That path is filled with the oddest surprises. The simple truths you thought you knew—like the grace of being truly forgiven, the possibility of being known and still loved—start to take shape inside you in ways that could not happen with all your plans in place.

> *The freedom to actually be on an adventure with God becomes strangely possible when you aren't pushing so hard for The Package.*

While you may take many trips over your life and unpack your literal suitcase a thousand times, there is really only one journey that matters—and that is the actual story that unfolds in learning to trust God as you share his company.

If your life worked out the way you think you want—or if you could just pretend that doesn't matter—it would all be easier. You might cruise into the sunset. But honestly, you'd miss out on a real journey with God.

And you'd walk right past wonderful.

*Chapter 2*

# THE DANGER OF SETTLING

## THE FEAR OF DISAPPOINTMENT
## CAN RULE YOUR LIFE

> *People who are most afraid of*
> *their dreams convince themselves*
> *they have no dreams at all.*
> —JOHN STEINBECK

> *My soul, wait silently for God alone,*
> *For my expectation is from Him.*
> —PSALM 62:5 NKJV

*2008*

*Not everyone is afflicted with great expectations.*

Many of us secretly believe that the safest path is the one where our hearts are kept on a tight leash. If we don't want much . . . we are seldom disappointed. A short wish list makes for an easier life—or so it seems. No one would accuse us of harboring great expectations. At some invisible place we don't even remember, we decided to aim low and to retreat from the risky places where our hearts might take a painful hit or two. We get good at settling. It's a familiar tale—one that thousands of us live—and if folks knew our real story, they would understand why.

When Allison was riding the roller coaster of hoping for a child and yet suffering through repeated miscarriages, I saw this temptation up close. We had many conversations about hope and expectation. Every empty month that rolled by meant another round of disappointment—and the inclination to despair. "You can't let go of hope, honey, just because you are disappointed," I would say. "You can't retreat into a cocoon of resignation."

Allison's response voiced what all of us have felt at some point. "But, Mom, it hurts to hope."

> *It takes faith to believe that if God says no to a good dream . . . it means God is up to something that will, eventually, have his glory written all over it.*

Do you know what she means? It takes such courage to stay awake to possibility—to keep bringing a hungry heart back to God, over and over, until he says it's time to let go. It takes faith to believe that if God says no to a good dream . . . it means God is up to something that will, eventually, have his glory written all over it. I find that trusting God with my life often leads to a place that's exhilarating and yet oddly painful at times. Indeed, it can hurt to hope.

It's crucial for us as women to realize the nature of the emotional path we walk with God. Our psyches are not formed like those of the men around us. We do actually feel

life more deeply. Recent neurological studies confirm what
we know intuitively: if someone wires a man and a woman
to a computer that measures
their internal responses as they
listen to the same sad story—
almost six times as many neu-
rons will be affected in the brain
of the woman. Bigger chunks
of our minds literally feel the
impact. Is it any wonder, then,
that when a close friend moves

*A hopeful heart is
absolutely vital to
experiencing the richness
and the wonder of the
journey God has for you.*

away or a cherished dream crumbles to bits, we are deeply
affected? Is it any surprise that we are tempted to find ways
to anesthetize our aching hearts?

That's why it's a lifelong challenge to live with a heart
that remains open to God and alive to possibility—even in
the face of disappointment. Yet a hopeful heart is absolutely
vital to experiencing the richness and the wonder of the journey God has for you.

The paradox here is that while it may hurt to hope, the
dangers of not hoping for much are far worse. In the oddest
sort of way, we tend to get what we hope for. You can see
this, for example, in the relational world of love and
romance. There the quandary of desire and expectation gets
played out in dramatic relief. For a woman soon learns that
if she expects too little from a man—too little is usually what
she'll get. The men who come her way will not be ones she
could build a life with. Having a clearer picture of what a

good man is and the courage to say, "Next!" to the ones who aren't is a starting point for finding a love that lasts.

Low expectations in love—as in so much of life—can spell disaster.

How, then, do we shut down our hearts? How do we shrink our expectations into such a compact size we can't be disappointed? We have a couple of tried-and-true ways. You might want to watch for these strategies in your own life, because they likely appear in your mind as utterly reasonable.

## LABELING OUR LONGINGS AS SELFISH

No woman with any grace or grit wants to think of herself as selfish. It feels like having a mustard stain smeared on a good white shirt and not knowing it. To be selfish is an awful label—and so, unfortunately, we often miss real selfishness in the subtle, relentless ways we maneuver others to get our way.

But wanting to be a mother who stays home with her children? Or longing for your husband to engage you in meaningful conversation? Or hoping that you can finally afford to knock out a wall and create some real elbow room for your family? Or desiring a job that gives your talents a chance to blossom? Or craving a day alone without anyone needing you? These desires are not selfish. Yet if I had a dollar for every time I've heard a woman label herself that way because she could not dare to believe her longings were possible, I could make a dent in world hunger.

If you hear yourself say, *I guess I'm just selfish to want . . .* , then let me encourage you: take a few moments and ask God, very simply, "Do you see my desire as selfish? And would you show me how to bring my longings to you and trust that you will give life to those—or that you will change that desire within me?"

I can almost guarantee that what you sense from God will not carry that edge of condemnation. You may even notice a greater sense of peace, a new ability to believe him in hard-to-believe places in your life. When we quickly pass off a desire as selfish, usually we are trying to get our hearts back into a tight, secure box . . . so we aren't disappointed.[1]

## LIVING ON PATROL

Some of us live with chronically low expectations because our energy is going elsewhere. We are busy patrolling the edges of our lives, fending off potential threats, managing our fears. We stopped dreaming long ago. If something tragic or repeatedly painful has happened in a woman's past, she can get stuck in the mode of merely protecting herself—but not really living and trusting God. All that energy goes into living as a border patrol.

The real problem with having low expectations, though, is that it runs so contrary to the way God has wired the universe. The angst of longing for something more is what makes us human—and what pulls us to God. He asks us to let him shape our desires—to purify and refine and hone them like sharp arrows. And then he gives the capacity to carry that hope within us until the time is right. Until his time is right. As Jesus said,

> *Ask* and it will be given to you;
> *seek* and you will find;
> *knock* and the door will be opened to you.
> (Matt. 7:7 NIV; emphasis added)

Notice how active those words are: *ask, seek,* and *knock.* Think of the way Jacob wrestled with God and God blessed his life—or the way David poured out his heart to the Lord (see Gen. 32; Ps. 32:34). There is some kind of truly interactive process when you bring the real desires of your heart to God and he literally reshapes your inner being. This journey you are on with God has all the pulls and tugs, ebbs and flows of a true relationship.

## THE DANGER IN DISAPPOINTMENT

The only way to keep your heart alive in the face of all that life throws your way is to decide that there are worse things than being disappointed. Our extraordinary efforts to keep from being hurt are mostly a waste of energy. Unfortunately, in a fallen world, disappointment is a given. It's more like a fact of life.

The really important part is where we go with an aching heart. The first time the totally unexpected happened in my life and I lost dreams and relationships that seemed irretrievable, I responded like many women do—I retreated into a quiet cocoon on the inside where no one could reach me. Not even God. And while I showed up where I needed to and kept the mechanics of a family going, I knew I was playing a role. I just couldn't name what was happening in me. For the first time ever, I found dust gathering on my Bible and the conversation with God shut down from my end.

> *The only way to keep your heart alive in the face of all that life throws your way is to decide that there are worse things than being disappointed.*

One morning before daybreak, I woke up early and a bit irritated that I was losing sleep on such a regular basis. As I lay there, I became aware of the presence of Jesus, sitting, as it were, at the foot of my bed. It was so real that I instinctively looked for the indention in the mattress. I had no category for this sort of experience, so it caught me unaware.

Before I could think further, though, very clearly and very simply words formed in my mind, so distinct they might as well have been audible.

*You are angry.*

I had to think about that for a minute. Southern women don't get angry—or at least, we often don't know it if we are.

*Hmm,* I said to myself, *maybe that's it; maybe I am angry*—rather surprised to be given a label for this shutdown place in which I was living.

Immediately, his response came as surely as if the words

were spoken. *Yes, you are angry . . . and if you'll let me walk with you through that, I'll bring you out the other side.*

I lay there and watched the sun come up, tears trickling down my face. I would never have believed that Jesus would meet me in such a way—or at such a messy, confused time in my life. I was amazed by his kindness. I could not—at that point—have let another living soul see the doubts and questions stirring in me and yet, somehow, God came after me in this dark place. He offered to bring me out the other side of whatever this was, and I knew I could not get there on my own.

Those small moments with God became a huge hinge in my life. Anger is often the face of loss and disappointment, like a doorway you have to go through to get to the real stuff. It's a hard scab on some wound in your heart that must be melted so the tender, vulnerable parts of you can know his touch.

> *You cry your tears and mourn what would have been . . . and slowly awaken to a new sense of hope for what might come in the place of what you lost.*

Naming my anger, then, was a path into the real grief of some very real losses. I learned for the first time what a cleansing thing grief can be. You cry your tears and mourn what would have been . . . and slowly awaken to a new sense of hope for what might come in the place of what you lost. Grief (which is often what's behind anger) washes your heart of ego and striving and leaves as a parting gift a new measure of humility. And even gratitude.

I love the way Anne Sexton writes about this in her poem, "Courage."

> Later,
> if you endured a great despair,
> then you did it alone,
> getting a transfusion from the fire,
> picking the scabs off your heart,
> then wringing it out like a sock.
> Next, my kinsman, you powdered your sorrow
> you gave it a back rub
> and then you covered it with a blanket
> and after it had slept a while
> it woke to the wings of roses
> and was transformed.[2]

Isn't that a wonderful picture of the way loss and disappointment can birth something new in our lives we would not have known otherwise? Personally, I doubt that, apart from God, much true transformation ever happens in the way it really could. For it is God who binds up the brokenhearted. He is the One who gives beauty for ashes, the grace to forgive and to be forgiven (Isa. 61:1–3). We have only to bring him the pieces.

Perhaps the richest part of this journey is discovering that God is not put off by a heart in bad need of repair. He, indeed, sits at the foot of our beds, waiting for us to recognize his presence where we least expect.

The danger in our lives is not that we'll be disappointed if we let our hearts off the leash—if we really step out there on the playing field and see where God takes us. The real thing to fear is that we'll try to manage disappointment on our own. I think, sometimes, of a woman who came up to me after I spoke and poured out her story—and how she mirrored the challenge we all face.

"My father died when I was young," she said, "and I lost my mother two years ago. My husband has seen one job after another come and go. I recently moved to this city, leaving behind the best friends I've ever had."

And then she paused and took a deep breath. "I fear I'm coming to see God as a Taker and not a Giver."

You can feel the way the enemy spots each of us in our most vulnerable moments and whispers in our ears something that seems true in isolation. *It's just you, honey, up against a cold, cruel world, and God is nowhere to be found. You have to make the best of it. Alone. You are all alone.*

> *The real thing to fear is that we'll try to manage disappointment on our own.*

So we bury our hearts in the backyard somewhere. We bundle up our angst and anxiety, our fear and our loss, into a neat package and *get on with it*. What dies on the inside, though, is some of the hope and expectation meant to fuel the journey. And we come to conclusions about God that are tragically inaccurate.

As I think of that first deep season of disappointment in my life when I felt things could never really be good again, I am strangely grateful. For God burst my categories—and they needed bursting. He insisted that I walk this out with him. Indeed, there was no other way through. And I discovered aspects of the love of Christ I would not have experienced in a million years. When I feel undone now, I'm not as easily fooled into believing I have to straighten it all up for God to be willing to join me.

I sometimes wonder where I would have gone on my own, trying to manage that loss myself. A picture floats across my mind that is way too close to true—the image of a woman who carved out her own notions about how to do life and became the worst of all adjectives: *bitter*.

## STRUGGLING WITH INTEGRITY

It's important to realize that wrestling through disappointment *with God* has a rich tradition in the Bible. Think of how David struggled with God as he hid out in caves and wondered aloud if, perhaps, God had forgotten him (see Ps. 13). Or Jeremiah, who admitted that he felt like God had driven him into darkness and made him live there. He survived by reminding himself of truth, in words we have come to love:

The LORD's lovingkindnesses indeed never cease,

For His compassions never fail.

They are new every morning;

Great is Your faithfulness. (Lam. 3:22–23)

The struggle itself is not some alien condition—as though we lost our spot on the victory train of spiritual success stories. The struggle is part of the relationship. It's what makes for intimacy.

When Jesus returned to the Father, he spoke words that touch the deepest emotional needs of our hearts: "I will come again . . . that where I am, there you may be also" (John 14:3). He is coming to take us home. And *home* is truly what we long for. In between now and then, however, we are following a trail of faith to a place we have not gone, led by Someone we have not met—in precise terms. Of course, we struggle to find our way.

On an emotional plane, there are two extremes on a continuum we call hope. We can live in a place of entitlement, with expectations that really belong in heaven. But the other possibility, and the one we've been exploring here, is just as ominous—that of settling. Just settling for whatever comes and asking for little else. Both extremes will pull you away from the rich opportunity of being on a journey with God and finding life in knowing—really knowing—him.

> *Wrestling through disappointment with God has a rich tradition in the Bible.*

Let me suggest that a third alternative exists. I would call it a place of acceptance. And real acceptance usually comes only on the far side of the actual emotional or spiritual struggle. It differs from plain old resignation in many ways. There is a fresh expectation that you will experience God's goodness, perhaps where you'd least think to look. You are not holding back on your life. In a strange way, you are more alive than ever. The future holds real promise.

When I think of integrity in the struggle—of acceptance without being resigned to something lesser than, I picture a woman named Nikki Das. As you may remember, a fighter jet did not return from the initial air campaign in the early stages of the war in Iraq. Nikki's husband, Eric Das, was piloting the two-man jet that did not return to base that night, for reasons no one has been able to determine.

If you could hear Nikki talk about her marriage to Eric, you'd know this relationship was one in a thousand. Eric was the kind of guy who seems a little too scarce these days— a talented Air Force Academy graduate and fighter pilot with a total zest for life, devoted to God, loyal to his last breath. And a man very much in love with

*The struggle is part of the relationship. It's what makes for intimacy.*

his wife. Together they served in the same air-force squadron —Eric was a pilot and Nikki, a squadron intelligence officer.

On Sunday, April 6, 2005, just before his seventeenth flight in Iraq, Nikki and Eric met for a few moments. They exchanged some mission details—and Eric stole one last quick kiss. "It never occurred to me that was the last time I'd see my husband alive. He was such a good pilot," Nikki explained. When Eric did not return, Nikki was lost in shock and disbelief. "It took two funerals, three memorials, and months of being alone to get it—my husband was not coming home."

By the time I met Nikki, she was a twenty-seven-year-old widow with a very different future from the one she had in mind. There was enormous grief in her life. Yet she didn't feel God had cut her a raw deal. She was not about to throw in the towel. "Honestly, it was a privilege to be Eric's wife," she told me more than once. She was grieving—but with bittersweet gratitude that she had gotten to share life with this man.

When a woman grieves her losses with integrity, she usually finds that her tears give way to a fresh sort of hope. She is not nearly as controlled by her fears because she's already faced something difficult head-on. Her future holds possibility that is not built on the ground of anything she was clinging to—except, perhaps, the promises of God.

## WHERE WONDERFUL BEGINS

In this dilemma of living somewhere between entitlement and resignation—of letting our hearts go on a real journey with God—there are two women in Scripture whose stories continually intrigue me.

Hannah is a favorite of any woman who has longed to be

a mother. You can see her pleading with God for a child, her heart so engaged she seems to be drunk. But she is not drinking; rather, she insists, her prayer is about her passionate longing for a child. "I have poured out my soul before the LORD," (1 Sam. 1:15) she says.

God gives her a son, Samuel, and with him the words that many a woman has claimed for the child of her prayers:

> "For this boy I prayed, and the LORD has given me my petition . . . So I have also dedicated him to the LORD; as long as he lives he is dedicated to the LORD." (1 Sam. 1:27–28)

Now notice how her story picks up in intensity. When Samuel is at the tender age of three, Hannah brings him back to the house of the Lord, where Eli will teach him what it means to serve God as a priest. Only Eli has failed miserably with his own sons, who are "worthless men," a disgrace to the priesthood (1 Sam. 2:12). Can you imagine how she felt leaving her small son to be cared for by this old man?

And what of Hannah's own dreams of being a mother and raising children? Hannah came once a year and brought Samuel a robe she'd made him, but she had no reason to think she would ever have another child.

What moves me about Hannah is the way she engaged God. Hers is that rare mixture of relentless hope and a surrendered heart. She asked God for the desire of her heart. And God asked her to do a very difficult thing with the gift of a son he gave.

I can never read the rest of her story without something melting inside me.

For as the saying goes, you can't outgive God. In the quaint words of the passage, "the LORD visited Hannah," and she gave birth to three more sons and two daughters (1 Sam. 2:21). Her son Samuel, who grew up in the care of an old priest, became the greatest judge in Israel's history.

I return to Hannah's story whenever I need to be reminded that God honors our willingness to hope. When we bring our desires and longings to Jesus, he does something remarkable with them. It may not look like what we had in mind—but we do not hope in vain. I think of Hannah when I have forgotten to remember that, often, real hardship is the front edge of God's blessing.

The other woman at whose feet I sit is Naomi. When we meet her in Scripture, she is no spring chicken. She's old and worn out, defeated by famine and the loss of her husband and two sons. She is tired of living in a strange place. She has one more move left in her—her feet are set on returning to Israel.

Ruth, her Moabite daughter-in-law, insists on returning with Naomi, wanting to start life over together. But Naomi, like all of us at some points, cannot see past her losses. Just call me "Mara," she says, which is a name that means "bitter." She is resigned to a bleak future. "The hand of the LORD has gone forth against me," she says (Ruth 1:13). That's how she sees her life. *Just get me home, and I'll ask for nothing more.*

Have you ever allowed a rough time in your life to tilt

your whole perspective? Do you find yourself reading your circumstances like tea leaves—and then misinterpreting your life? That was Naomi's story, and that's why the rest of the story is so encouraging.

But God has more in mind for Naomi than she knows. For Ruth is going to marry Boaz. Ruth, the human embodiment of all Naomi has lost, is the woman through whom God will give Naomi something she would never have dreamed. A son is born—Naomi's grandson—the gift of her old age, a child who rocks in her lap and nestles in her wrinkled arms.

As the light fades on the stage of Naomi's life, that's exactly where we are left—watching this defeated woman smile again. God does not leave her in some hopeless place she was only too willing to accept. For the story behind the story is this: the child she cradles is the grandfather of David, the father of the father of the father . . . of Jesus Christ. Naomi is the woman in Scripture whose life says, "Hold on, there's a bigger story." *There's a bigger story.*

*Oh, Lord,* I find myself praying, *let me look past the smoke from the ashes of my dreams and expectations until I find you.*

So I ask God to keep my soul closer to that of Hannah's. I would rather live with a heart that is repeatedly poured out before the Lord, even if it's painful. And when I fall into Naomi's snare of just settling because I cannot believe God would meet me in this difficulty, then I pray my eyes would be opened to see what he might put in my own lap—because he is that good.

I am pleased to tell you that Allison, the daughter who wanted to give up hope, did eventually, after lots of waiting and wondering, have a son herself. His name is Andrew. His toddler smile lights up a room just as he sets about to demolish it. There are worlds out there to conquer, and he is starting early. He can't imagine how much he was prayed for.

I look at Andrew's face, not yet old enough to grow its mask, and I see all the wonder still in place. A simple geranium is a great delight. A bug on the driveway merits careful analysis. I stand him up in the driver's seat of my parked Jeep and he grabs the wheel with a huge grin, like he is Richard Petty in diapers. He literally squeals for joy.

Andrew mirrors the thing I most want to hold on to in this journey with Christ—the wonder. *Oh, Lord,* I find myself praying, *let me look past the smoke from the ashes of my dreams and expectations until I find you.*

For Christ is—as the parable claims—the treasure hidden in a field, worth selling all we own to possess. And living your real life *with him* is, truly, where wonderful begins.

*Chapter 3*

# DISTURBING INTERRUPTIONS

## GOD CHOOSES SUCH
## UNEXPECTED PATHS

> *That is the great conversion in our life: to recognize
> and believe that the many unexpected events are
> not just disturbing interruptions of our projects, but the way
> in which God molds our hearts and prepares us for his return.*
> —HENRI NOUWEN

> *Dear friends, do not be surprised at the painful trial you are
> suffering, as though something strange were happening to you.*
> —1 PETER 4:12 NIV

*The challenge in all our notions of wonderful is that God may* have a different sort of wonderful than the one we have in mind. As the saying goes, life happens while you are busy making plans. Henri Nouwen called the unexpected and the unwanted by this name: disturbing interruptions of our projects. That is exactly how it feels—as though God might be intervening in our lives, but in ways we hardly recognize.

I think of a friend, Angie, for whom disturbing interruption came in the form of panic attacks. Sometimes, anxiety is like Morse code tapping out a message we may not be able to hear another way. It can be a woman's first clue that she needs to slow down and take some time to listen to her life.

Angie taught sixth grade—a job that would give lots of people extreme anxiety. But Angie loved teaching. She was mystified by the panic attacks.

"This is maddening," Angie would complain to me. "I've been teaching for ten years. Why this? Why now?"

Teaching was a natural fit for her. Most of the women in her family had been teachers. Yet I felt the need to ask her if there was something else she wanted to do—was there somewhere else she wanted to be at this point in her life?

She thought about it for a long moment. "I worry about not being at home with my own children, to tell the truth," she said with a tinge of embarrassment. She knew she was missing simple, relaxed moments with two children, who would never be small again. Yet she was afraid of the loss of income her husband counted on—and even more, she feared the loss of identity. She was a teacher, a woman with a place in a school and people who counted on her. Who would she be if she came home?

I encouraged her to take a simple question and make it part of her prayer life for a while. "Lord, what is this anxiety telling me about what I really believe about myself . . . and about you?" Don't feel like you have to force an answer, I told her. Just lay the question out before God for a period of time and see what comes to you.

After a number of weeks, Angie found that she woke up

one morning from a dream she could barely remember, yet the words formed in her mind were clear as a bell. *I am a mistake.* She knew immediately that statement fit. It matched the missing piece in the puzzle of her heart exactly. Angie had been born to parents who married under the duress of pregnancy and, years later, divorced. She was the reason her father gave up his law-school dream to work in a car plant in Detroit, like his dad before him.

On a heart level, her anxiety attacks made so much sense. Of course, she felt driven to prove herself. She'd lived like a butterfly pinned to the wall—without the internal permission to explore and weigh out possibilities, without much chance to fly. Without the option to leave it all behind for a while and come home.

If you believe you are a mistake, you put your head down and keep walking—until God, in his mercy, intervenes in one of those disturbing interruptions.

## STIRRING UP OUR NESTS

Isn't it strange the way God works in our lives? Who would think that he would use something physical, like anxiety, to expose a place of spiritual bondage—and to invite us into the freedom in him we would not have known?

I still find myself surprised by the trouble God goes to in order to spring the lock on our souls. In weaker moments, I have wanted God to be more like a cruise director on a Carnival ship headed for the Bahamas—rather than the One who spoke the worlds into being and who pledged himself in Christ to shape holiness into my heart. I would wish to be less disturbed. Or as the philosopher Søren Kierkegaard once said, "If you desire, humanly speaking, pleasant and happy days, then never get seriously involved with Christ."[1]

Perhaps it's harder for us to recognize the fingerprints of God in difficult places of our journey because God's parenting has a deeper goal than our own. As good mothers, we move heaven and earth to prevent our children from experiencing pain. I remember one mother who claimed she would fight a buzz saw with her bare hands to make life easier for her children. Maybe you wouldn't exactly fight a buzz saw, but I'm sure you know what she means. We want to spare our children every distress we can.

So it's understandable that along our journey we have to be reminded that God is a different sort of Father. He wounds—in order to heal. He dismantles and exposes, so that we might know his cleansing love in the deeper reaches of our being. The Old Testament uses the metaphor of an eagle to describe the kind of parent God is:

> "Like an eagle that stirs up its nest,
> That hovers over its young,
> He spread His wings and caught them,
> He carried them on His pinions." (Deut. 32:11)

An eagle knows the moment when the time is right to nudge his baby bird over the side of the nest—into a panicky free fall through thin air. Then he swoops beneath this fluttering mess of feathers. He catches his young and carries her on his pinions to safety until, little by little, this bird learns she has eagle's wings too. She can fly.

Do you know what it's like to have your nest stirred—or to feel like some new challenge has thrown you way out of your comfort zone? Our faith journey will never make much sense until we can trace the hand of God behind it all.

*I still find myself surprised by the trouble God goes to in order to spring the lock on our souls.*

In his book *The Problem of Pain*, C. S. Lewis wrote that God whispers to us in our pleasures, but he shouts to us in our pains. Over the rumblings of your anxiety or your fear or your disappointment, can you make out some part of what he's saying to you?

## SAVING US FROM OURSELVES

Perhaps the natural question we ask is more like, "What is God up to?" How is it that this journey with him so often takes us down paths we would not have chosen—and many times, right into the middle of situations we have worked half a life to avoid?

Years ago, while my husband was finishing seminary, we took a summer to visit ministries in England and Holland. We were still fighting jet lag the morning we met with a British pastor—an older gentleman who peered over his glasses at us as though we'd recently escaped from the Colonies. I have never forgotten the question he asked me.

"So, Paula, what pit did God dig you out of?" he said, leveling his gaze on me.

My Southern sensibilities labeled that a rather tacky thing to say, and thankfully, the jet lag kept me from responding. Then it struck me: *This man is speaking to me from Psalm 40.* As the words rolled through my head, I understood what he was asking.

> I waited patiently for the LORD;
> And He inclined to me, and heard my cry.
> He brought me up out of the pit of destruction,
>     out of the miry clay;
> And He set my feet upon a rock making my
>     footsteps firm.
> He put a new song in my mouth, a song of
>     praise to our God;
> Many will see and fear,
> And will trust in the LORD. (vv. 1–3)

He was asking, in a lovely, poetic way, how God had gotten hold of me. What miry clay, what pit of mud had God dug me out of, indeed?

I have realized the deep truth of those words through the years—God is even yet in the process of digging us out of the pit of destruction. We come into this world with a particular set of snares and insecurities that lead us into choices that are plain old sin. And this mud hole is where our hearts too easily return. The mercy of God is that he comes after us, relentlessly saving us from our very own pit.

It's rather like an observation a good friend made one day, as he reflected on his life. He's a well-loved pediatrician in the Midwest and the father of two children. His son went to an Ivy League school—the kind of child who won an array of awards. But his daughter has multiple handicaps and a whole list of problems. It's been a twenty-year struggle. In a moment of stunning clarity, he said, "You know, I realize that without my daughter I would have been a pompous prig. In so many ways, God has been saving me from myself."

*God has been saving me from myself.* Oh, how true those words are. The longer I am on this journey, the more I understand their meaning. God does intend to save us from ourselves. He stirs up the careful nests we've gathered—and sometimes, that is worse than uncomfortable.

## OLD WAYS OF COPING

We grow up assembling a secret little bag of skills and aptitudes that work for us. They take us places. They bring us applause. Perhaps you learned to hide in your bedroom and bury yourself in a book while your parents fought like cats and dogs in the living room. That strategy helped you survive when you were ten years old. It might have even made you an ace student.

But if we carry old survival skills way into our adulthood, they either don't work as well—or they backfire. A woman who hides in her room as an adult often finds she has missed her life. Everything that matters to her—her relationships, her desires, her purpose in life—is happening out there in the living room, so to speak. She has to let go of the old safe places.

God has designed the universe so as to push us out of our comfort zones. We have to step off the side of the nest and fly, even if it feels like a free fall for a while. That naked place of risky newness is the only place we learn to trust him. As the Lord shares through the pen of Isaiah,

> "I will lead the blind by a way they do not know,
> In paths they do not know I will guide them
> I will make darkness into light before them
> And rugged places into plains
> These are the things I will do,
> And I will not leave them undone." (Isa. 42:16)

## OTHER SAVIORS

The more we understand our own particular pit of destruction, the more clearly we see our secret dependencies. What we lean on—what we count on—often isn't God at all. It's our family connections or our savings account or the way we look. Until the wrinkles set in deeply or as long as our family stays intact, we don't even know we are leaning the weight of our lives on those things.

Growing up with a younger brother who was always a ten-ton gorilla (he went to college on a football scholarship), I learned how to talk my way out of close encounters. Well-chosen words could be quite persuasive in a pinch. A carefully laid-out argument was often just the trump card I needed.

It works . . . until you find yourself sitting by the bedside of a very sick friend and your words are worse than useless. Or your child is determined to do it his way and he is singularly unimpressed with your flawless logic. Until the things that matter deeply cannot be gotten by a fresh new idea well put. What you see as a strength suddenly seems impotent. They're only words.

You can find yourself at a huge loss in those moments when something you've counted on evaporates into thin air. We all have our secret dependencies.

God speaks into those through the words of Isaiah. He says, "I, even I, am the LORD, and *there is no savior besides Me*" (Isa. 43:11; emphasis added). Our journey with the Lord is often a series of experiences in which we are startled into some deeper awareness that only God will see us through. *Only God.*

As that happens, we are more able to use a talent—without depending on it. We can love someone without seeing him as the source of life. We have only one, true Savior.

## ANCIENT LIES

One pattern in all our stories emerges with stunning predictability—like some drama being staged over and over. Somewhere along the way, we usually run square into something we have long feared.

The woman who won all the prizes early in her life encounters failure—or at least it feels like failure to her. Or the woman who's a master at forging relationships discovers that the love of her life or her firstborn child wants his space. He may move three time zones away to get it. And suddenly, she finds herself pulling the splinters of rejection out of her heart.

I can still picture a woman in the engulfing pain of a husband who left her for another woman after two years of marriage. Sarah had known Ben since high school. Her best memories were centered on him. His rejection left her feeling paralyzed, as though she could not walk out her door alone. She'd lost her father much earlier through his addiction to alcohol; the losses were stacking up inside her.

*It's the lie inside the loss that will determine our future.*

"How do you see your husband's leaving?" I asked her, trying to understand how she was interpreting such a painful event. "What is that about?"

"When Ben walked out the door, he took *me* with him," she responded. "His leaving told me what I knew all along— I don't matter. I've never mattered to a man. Whatever I have to give is not good enough."

I could understand why Sarah felt she couldn't leave her house. She was paralyzed by rejection that had ignited the most painful parts of her past.

While a loss like the one Sarah experienced is a great grief, it's the lie inside the loss that will determine her future. A woman can't live the life she's meant to—or one that honors God—when she secretly believes she has to wait for a man to love her well in order to really matter. She is somebody when he smiles at her—and nobody much when he's gone. That kind of lie is an emotional prison sentence.

## SPRINGING THE LOCK

When bondage in a woman's life (or in my own) becomes apparent, I feel the strangest sort of hope. I know that God is after something good. God begins to dismantle our old ways of coping, and when he pries our sticky fingers off the things we trust instead of him, when he exposes a lie that has ruled our lives—we are standing square in the center of his love. God is both beautiful and severe, as singer Derek Webb writes.[2] When God takes the lid off our lives in this way, it's a mercy. A great, good, and severe mercy.

Oh, for the words to communicate a love willing to come after us in this way! C. S. Lewis called God's willingness to bruise in order to heal "an intolerable compliment." He means that God's care for us is expressed in all the trouble he goes to in shaping our souls. He is like an artist who is passionate about a painting he is laboring over. Lewis writes,

> In the same way, it is natural for us to wish that God had designed for us a less glorious and less arduous destiny; but then we are wishing not for more love, but for less.[3]

Admittedly, this intolerable compliment, this severe mercy, can feel like being squeezed through an hourglass. Angie found her panic attacks maddening. But she is grateful to have discovered a purpose for her life that transcends her parents' story or her role as a teacher. Sarah wouldn't wish divorce on anyone. Yet it was the place where she first asked God to speak truth into her heart. *Who am I, really? How do you feel about me, Lord? What does it mean to love a man without finding my life in him?*

Wherever there is bondage in our lives, there is also a distorted image of God. It's as though some part of us is still tied in knots. Think of how that distortion may be revealed in your life:

- If you find it hard to receive love from others . . . you may also view God as aloof and removed, as though he is always waiting to see if you make the grade.

- When you live in a chronically angry, critical place, it's usually because you see God as being angry and aloof with you.

- When you're controlled by your fears, the power of God is just a spiritual phrase that gets tossed around. But it's not really something you rest your heart upon.

- If you find it nearly impossible to forgive someone who's wronged you, you likely have experienced little of God's forgiveness yourself.

For all these reasons, then, God comes after us. Over and over and over the work of the Holy Spirit is felt in our lives, digging us out of a pit of destruction until we can stand on the truth.

Disillusionment, then, is a necessary rite of passage. It's the letting go of our illusions about ourselves—and especially about God.

## THE WISDOM TO CLING

A few weeks before our son was scheduled to complete the four years of flight training necessary to become a commercial pilot, he developed an ordinary case of hives. The doctor recommended an antihistamine available in any drugstore, taken by hundreds of people daily. But for Brady, that same medication proved toxic.

My husband was in South America when I got a phone call. "Please come to Florida immediately—your son needs medical attention." When I arrived, I took one look at Brady and knew he'd had a bad reaction to something. And a bad reaction to anything can spell the end of flying planes. I knew this would take weeks to sort out—with Brady's dream of being a pilot left hanging in the balance.

Brady had wanted to be a pilot since he was a child. He'd made huge sacrifices to get this training. The thought, then, that he might lose his dream caused me no small amount of anxiety.

I did something I had never done before in quite this way. I chose three psalms that spoke to my fears.[4] Then morning and noon and night for weeks on end, I stopped what I was doing and prayed through one of these passages. These psalms sat there, like old friends—waiting for me, helping me to trust God.

I began to realize that as every week passed, I was noticeably calmer. I was starting to exhale again. The comfort of God was a little more real each day. Bit by bit I could actually believe what I knew was true—whatever turn this took for Brady, God would be there. God loved my son more than I did.

There are times when we cling to God in the fog, and certainly, this was one of those for me. What I realize, though, as I look back in this journey with God is that nearly everything that's valuable and real to me has come from just this sort of clinging. Other people can tell us a lot of helpful things about God. Reading a book has its place. In the long run, though, the real stuff comes from crawling your way back to the watering hole of his grace, over and over again.

What's yours—what you own—is what you reach for of God in those moments where the bottom of life has dropped out. Your experience of God in those seasons becomes the real source of wonder.

In this pilgrimage of faith, there are problems and difficulties in which we experience God's true deliverance. Today, my son is flying planes all over the country. The first time I picked him up from the airport in his official pilot's uniform, I could have wept for joy.

My gratitude comes from knowing the other side of reality. It could easily have gone the other way. I have traveled far enough to realize there are obstacles in our paths that God allows to remain in place—year after year after year. In spite of all the prayer. No matter how hard we work. Some things just refuse to yield. Like every woman I know well, I can point to difficult relationships or health problems or financial challenges that are . . . well, just *there* in my life—like annoying passengers that insist on coming along for the trip.

*Could this disturbing interruption of my plans be the actual way God is molding my heart in some new manner?*

It's a bit of a mystery what God chooses to remove from your life—and what he allows to remain. You cannot help but ask for that heartache, that nagging difficulty, to go away.

But if it remains . . . what will you do, then?

I've come to believe that we all carry an invisible pendulum inside us. For the longest time, it seems, the weight of our prayer is a plea for God to remove some particular problem. *Lord, please take this away.* And, indeed, sometimes he does. The child is healed. The business recovers, and we are grateful.

But when the challenge remains—when it insists on coming along for the trip—the great question inside us swings in a new direction. Might this thing I long to be different be the actual crucible on which God chooses to shape my soul into something of beauty that perhaps only he sees? Could this disturbing interruption of my plans be the actual way God is molding my heart in some new manner? *Will I let God transform me in this?*

I often wish there was an easier path. But honestly, I doubt if we can experience Christ in any way that matters, by any lesser means.

This process of encountering God in ways we do not expect—of being loved by him according to his definition of love—is a rite of passage for each of us.

When at least a few of your dreams don't work out, you are at a new place with him. When disillusionment strips you of your illusions, you may be in a position to receive what he has wanted to give all along. When you start to feel as though you're not sure who God is anymore, often you are on the verge of discovering the God you never knew but who always was —and has only been, somehow, shrouded by your preconceptions.

> *What you've always heard about God is really true—you are loved beyond your wildest imaginings.*

This is the juncture in the journey where the richness of the gospel slowly begins to come alive. What you've always heard about God is really true—you are loved beyond your wildest imaginings. There is a place of rest in God that releases you from endless fretting. Christ's compassion can be felt in your worst moments. It is truly better than your dreams.

We can never really discover that, though, as long as our hearts are stapled to the life we think should be ours.

# FINDING YOUR STUCK PLACES

*Surely you desire truth in the inner parts;*
*you teach me wisdom in the inmost place.*
—PSALM 51:6 NIV

Most of us realize that what we believe, down deep, determines how we actually live. But *getting at that* can be an issue. This is where our perennial fears, the *stuck places* in our lives, the behaviors we can't seem to change can provide important keys to understanding our own journey in God.

Take a few minutes and a blank sheet of paper. Ask God to guide you and to bring understanding you cannot get on your own. Ask him to take you to a troublesome memory . . . a significant fear . . . a relationship that bothers you . . . or a choice you keep making that feels *choiceless.* Simply see what God brings to your mind as you pray.

Then, without analyzing or critiquing your words, write in free-flow fashion about the stuck place God brings to mind.

What are you feeling as you write?

What are you afraid of losing? What do you fear can never be yours unless . . .?

In the midst of that . . . what are you really believing about God?

Stay with what you've written without judging yourself harshly (as it's not the point). If this place of unbelief and fear in your heart was a little girl who's scared to death of something . . . then what does that little girl need to hear from God?

You can close this simple exercise by using what God's shown you to pray like a daughter would talk to her Father about the actual emotional place where you feel, on some level, lost and alone. What do you need? What do you feel led to ask of your Father?

When you run into this particular fear . . . or difficult relationship . . . or failure in the future, return to this place with God and ask him what he wants to show you. Ask him for the next right step.

# THE REAL ADVENTURE

*Chapter 4*

# OWNING YOUR STUFF

GRACE THAT ALLOWS YOU
TO COME CLEAN

*Before God can deliver us we must undeceive ourselves.*
—AUGUSTINE

*Therefore let us draw near with confidence
to the throne of grace, so that we may receive
mercy and find grace to help in time of need.*
—HEBREWS 4:16

*Chris was a capable woman who led the children's program* in a large church. What no one knew, though, was that Chris was also addicted to prescription pain medication. A severe neck injury and the stress of her life combined to grease the skids for a slow slide into drug dependence. By the time I met her, she was spending huge sums of money ordering painkillers off the Internet, without her doctor's knowledge. Living in the hazy world of addiction, Chris was very much alone.

"Perhaps now is the time to step down from your position,

tell your pastoral staff, and get some help for this," I suggested gently. "People rarely get past a drug dependence alone. It's a real battle."

Just the thought that others would know her struggle was more than Chris could bear. She could beat this if she tried hard, surely she could. Her order this month was less than the month before—she was making progress. And then she added a comment that stopped me short.

"Besides, I'm living under grace," she said. "And grace means that I'm forgiven, so I don't have to tell."

I took a deep breath. "No," I replied. "Grace means that because you are loved, you can come clean."

Coming clean. Being forgiven. Owning your stuff. How do we account for the miracle, really, of this great, wide mercy in Christ that allows us to name the worst about ourselves—and still be loved? What do we make of a grace that insists the truth can be told when it needs to be?

*The ability to* own your stuff *with God and with others is the wildest freedom on the planet.*

When I hear the worship song "I Stand in Awe of You," this is my own picture of awe —that in Jesus there is the capacity to actually face myself, realizing God knows even better than I do what a gap there is, at times, between what I profess . . . and what I can pull off. He knows how easily I can be seduced into thinking there is a more attractive life out there than the one I'm living with him. He *knows* me . . .

and still welcomes me to his banquet table. *Yes, God, I stand in awe of you.*

But there is more. For the very mercy that gives us a place in the Father's love even when our soul is in shambles holds something more: we get the chance to exhale in the presence of others. You can stop trying so hard to keep up the appearance of this woman who has all her flaws tucked in (which, of course, they never are). The possibility of being human—being real with others—comes into view. You get to be at home in your own skin, able to offer a relationship to others that is more than just peeking out from behind a mask. *Oh, what a relief.*

I am convinced that being on a journey with the Lord down this rather narrow path leads to an incredibly spacious place. The ability to *own your stuff* with God and with others is the wildest freedom on the planet. And it is possible in Christ in ways that psychology and self-help and wishful thinking cannot begin to touch.

## SPIRITUAL ADULTERY

Let me describe the process of owning my own stuff from an episode in my life that occurred at the height of my disappointment with God. It is not unlike the stories of countless other women I've known through the years.

When you are disappointed and not quite able to walk through that experience with God, you are open prey. Which is what I was. What came along and began to fascinate the socks off me was Jungian psychology. Not prone to half-efforts, I bought every book I could lay my hands on. As my children entertained themselves on a McDonald's playground various mornings, I sat inside sipping coffee, trying to discover which archetype I was missing and what exactly were my animus and anima.

I was a woman in a trance, fascinated with this hidden world that felt like being handed a travel guide to a sort of secret knowledge of my inner being—a blueprint of the unseen machinations of my heart.

One shade of my disappointment, then, was the fear that following Jesus would lead to a life cast in tones of dull sepia—with the strength and flavor, say, of weak coffee in a Styrofoam cup. That was my own delusion. In some bare-bones way I was questioning if there was something out there more real than my Christian faith. Is Jesus *really* life?

*Could it be that what I'm really seeking is there waiting to be discovered in Jesus, and I've overlooked it?*

Savoring Carl Jung's ideas is not exactly running off with the postman, you might say. This is true. Yet affairs of the heart are just as ruinous as affairs of the flesh. And as I studied, I could sense my heart moving away from Christ and toward something else, God only knew what. I was being seduced by the illusion of control (as I realized years later). *If you know and understand . . . you can keep from being hurt.* You can control your life. Whatever form that illusion takes, it's the most powerful of all seductions.

God would not leave me there, though, sipping my coffee and reading myself comatose. Something about this was disquieting. It made me want to hide those books under my mattress. Jung blurred distinctions—he blended good and evil into one pile of mush. You can't worship Christ as God and yet be on a search for your own divinity, as he suggests. Jung's philosophy held a strong pull, though I was troubled by it. I could sense, as I read, that down this path lay the lure of another god.[1]

The turning point came one day when a verse I had not thought about in years suddenly came to me as I was reading: ". . . Christ Himself, *in whom are hidden all the treasures of wisdom and knowledge*" (Col. 2:2–3; emphasis added). The phrase stopped me short. I wondered, *Could it be that what I'm really seeking is there waiting to be discovered in Jesus, and I've overlooked it?*

I don't know if God replies with the word, *Bingo!* but he might as well have. I started to suspect how shallow my understanding of the faith really was. I wanted, badly, to be a woman who was fully alive, with access to everything that was real on the inside. It was as though God leaned across the table and said, *Honey, I'm the only One who can take you there.*

You may think as you read how much this response sounds like the way Jesus spoke to the woman at the well who'd had five husbands and was looking for love in all the wrong places. He did not condemn her desire for love (that is important).

But he said in no uncertain terms, *Come to me.* "Whoever drinks of the water that I will give him shall never thirst; but the water that I will give him will become in him a well of water springing up to eternal life" (John 4:14).

God was saying something like that to me, and I turned my attention to him in a new way, with a sense of expectancy I had not had before. I closed my books, got my children off the playground, and began to go home—in the deepest sense of the word.

> *Even children of light can be amazingly blind at times.*

Whenever I look back on this era of my life, it still grieves me a bit that being steeped in the Bible did not prevent such a seduction of soul. But many women echo such sentiments. *How could I not see where that affair would lead? Why didn't I realize my words would estrange my daughter-in-law for years? How have I let the need to keep everyone happy and pleased rule my life?*

Even children of light can be amazingly blind at times.

## COMING HOME

I have told my own prodigal story here because I'm convinced that we all have places in our lives like this. Some other love or loyalty moves in on us . . . and we give a piece of our hearts away. A passion other than Christ captures us. It truly is like being seduced, even for a season. I sometimes wonder how I can have journeyed this long with the Lord—and still feel pulled or intrigued or fascinated by anything else. But I can.

We all can, actually.

My point is not to wallow in the awfulness of a heart gone astray, in its various physical and spiritual forms. It is awful. And it grieves the heart of God because we're cheating on the best love there is. But that is not exactly my focus.

My real point is that the farther you go in this journey with the Lord, the more you will see about your own heart. As you step deeper into his love, that profound acceptance makes it possible to actually face the unvarnished truth about yourself—and yet not drown in shame. I would call that *owning your stuff*. The Bible uses an old and lovely word: *repentance*. It means to do an about-face—to make a choice to go in a new direction.[2]

Scripture tells us that we are led here, to a place of repentance, by the kindness of God (see Rom. 2:4). This pull on our hearts is one of the primary ways in which God loves us. As a wise old monk from Downside Abbey, England, once wrote (emphasis added):

> The gospel confession of sin is the most generous, secure, adventurous expression of the human heart. It is the risk that is only taken in the certainty of being acceptable and accepted. It is the full and final expression of that confidence. Only to your lover do you expose your worst. *To an amazed world Jesus presents a God who calls for this confession only so that he may reveal himself in a person's depths as his lover.*[3]

God gives us glimpses into our flawed hearts—not to shake his finger in our face, but to draw us, as a lover would, into his exclusive embrace. It's this taste of his love that makes all other loves pale in comparison.

However we might describe it, the best snapshot of our hearts is captured in the story of the prodigal son and the elder brother. The father had two sons, and each of them is being invited to live—to be at home—in the father's love.

## THE PRODIGAL

The younger son represents all those choices—the moments and the seasons—when the experience of any far country looks better to us than the life God offers. It may be as subtle as the example I gave, where a new philosophy appears to shimmer with hope and promise. Or you may recognize something more concrete in a search for love that takes you to a person or an activity that feels like leaving home.

As Henri Nouwen writes in his well-loved book on these two brothers, "I leave home every time I lose faith in the voice that calls me the Beloved and follow the voices that offer a great variety of ways to win the love I so much desire."[4]

## THE ELDER BROTHER

It's much harder to find oneself as the elder brother though. He looks so good, working hard on his father's estate. Who would guess his heart is a secret cauldron of anger and jealousy? Why, the very idea that his father would throw his good-for-nothing younger brother a party! "All these years

I've been slaving for you and never disobeyed your orders. Yet you never gave me even a young goat so I could celebrate with my friends," he whines (Luke 15:29 NIV).

We live as the elder brother when we see our obedience as a burden and our service as slavery. "I have to . . . I ought to . . . I should," we keep telling ourselves—but deep down, we doubt that God will do right by us. The elder brother's complaint comes "from a heart that feels it never received its due."⁵

*The farther you go in this journey with the Lord, the more you will see about your own heart.*

I think of a friend named Tate whose father died in a car accident, leaving her mother to raise three children alone. She and her sister were close in age—they had many of the same friends. They competed in school. My friend felt she could never get the attention of her overwhelmed mother to be seen and known for who she was, as Tate.

She slowly realized that she lived like that with God too— as his dutiful daughter who felt unrecognized, as though there wasn't enough love to go around. For Tate to leave the inner place of the elder brother was to let herself believe that God had a place at the table of his favor set just for her—that he knew her intimately with a love warmer and more inviting than the best mother. She did not have to live in this striving, envious, clamoring-for-approval place so familiar to her.

When I think of repentance as a change of heart, I picture it as waking up on the inside . . . and then coming home, like the prodigal who returned to his father empty-handed or the elder brother who may have finally realized that he was refusing to join the party. It's really the freedom to name what is actually happening in your own heart. *You become aware*—of the joke you made at someone's expense. Of the secret envy you feel for a friend whose life seems plush and easy. Of the impatience that bubbles up when you are tired of serving a difficult person who rarely says thank you.

You wake up and become aware—and the fact that you can hear a voice calling you home is the mercy of God.

## LIVING UNDER THE MERCY

What I hope you hear in this, at the roots of your being is the preposterous willingness of God to meet you wherever you are . . . and to bring you home. Maybe you haven't opened a Bible in fifteen years. Perhaps you've thought of leaving your husband and no one knows. Or maybe your love for God has become so dishrag dull you understand full well how attractive a new shade of psychology could be. When you hear the phrase *owning your stuff*, what actually comes to mind?

We get honest with God (or anyone, really) as we come to hope that what awaits is not his judgment but his kindness. The love of God always comes with a bit of surprise. We've never been loved like that, not even close. There is no one in the universe who knows us to such depths—and yet embraces us in a love as vast as the mercy that flows from the cross of Christ.

Yet few of us live in the light of that acceptance. Brennan Manning, who writes about intimacy with God, once noted that the obstacles to experiencing that seem different for men and women. Men, he claims, are more often held back by their own pride. But women? What keeps us distant and aloof and believing we have to handle things ourselves? After years of offering spiritual direction to many folks, Brennan believes that women fall prey to their own self-contempt. We tend to condemn ourselves—and then live in the emotional and spiritual isolation of our own prison cells.[6]

Most of us don't go there with God because in our hearts we believe that God is just like us—that is, he's waiting to read off a litany of complaints and reprimands. "You thought I was altogether like you," God says (Ps. 50:21 NIV). Meaning, of course, that since I would mark my name off the list of favored children, God would all the more.

*What I hope you hear in this, at the roots of your being is the preposterous willingness of God to meet you wherever you are . . . and to bring you home.*

"Therefore there is now no condemnation for those who are in Christ Jesus," the apostle Paul writes in Romans 8:1. How often have you heard that verse—at a funeral or in a sermon, perhaps? Have you ever really heard those words in your personal life, though—in the sealed-off places in your own heart that no one can see?

As the old expression goes, "There are parts of me that have never heard the gospel." This is so true. If I let the love and forgiveness of God into those corners of my soul, *no condemnation* means that I see God waiting for me—not with a scowl on his face but with arms that embrace a daughter who knows she is home.

Listen to the refreshing, intimate way one man describes such a moment with God when he realized his own sin. He writes:

> I am overwhelmed by the utterly spare truthfulness of these things, as God has shown them to me without rancor, *without condemnation.* And I feel strangely relieved, cleansed, and unburdened. To have seen these things with Him, and not in opposition to Him—I see them simply falling away, out of my life (emphasis added).[7]

That God would love us in our shame—that he would sit with you as he sat with me under the golden arches of McDonald's and offer to lead you into the essence of what you may be searching for in many futile places . . . who ever expects to be loved like this? His kindness is, truly, a wonder—and it is the very thing that makes it possible for our lives to change.

## THE POWER TO CHANGE

It's easy at this point to sell the gospel short. The grace in God's forgiveness includes the power to change. The love of

God exposes what's within—not to condemn us but to clean up our act. His forgiveness is the beginning of real life change, but it's not the end.

I have met many women who feel caught in a destructive pattern they feel powerless to change. It is not enough to say that Christ forgives. Can he also give the grace to take hard steps in a new direction? Will he meet me when I am alone and feeling desperate, and I want to give in to what I know has worked for me in the past? Is his love *that* real?

I think of Cindy (and many other women) whose earliest memories of feeling close to someone were sexual ones. By the time her parents completed their angry divorce, Cindy had discovered that the arms of a guy could wrap her in a cocoon of comfort—for a little while, at least. Throw in some alcohol, and she could make the world go away.

*The grace in God's forgiveness includes the power to change.*

By the time Cindy finished college, this pattern was so entrenched she could hardly imagine a friendship with a man that didn't become sexual.

Except that somewhere in it all, Cindy became a Christian. So now, she felt *bad* when she slept with a guy. She had no words for the shame and desperation that drove her on to the next man.

What was missing for her was forgiveness made concrete. Her life began to change when she let Christ walk her into new places—like a circle of girlfriends and someone to call when she felt desperate enough to pick up a guy. She would tell you that Christ's power in her life is that she's learning to share *herself*, rather than her body. Slowly she's begun to experience close relationships with men that don't ever turn sexual.

Each of us is Cindy in some way. We return to the same sources of comfort . . . until they control us. When Christ says that he has come to give us life, he means that he intends to love us out of every false refuge, no matter how long we've called that home. It is a tender mercy—but it's a rather painful love.

## TO BE FORGIVEN

In the remote countryside a few hours outside of Moscow lives a medical doctor named Lydia, who oversees the care for an orphanage full of children. If you walked through the door of this huge, rambling building on the banks of the Volga River, you would be swarmed by sweet-faced, intelligent children looking up at you, eyes pleading. Most are there because of bed-wetting and the neglect of alcoholic parents.

Lydia's own story, which takes place in the waning days of the Soviet State, often comes to mind when I think of the power of forgiveness in our lives. Lydia desired to help these children but had scant resources, so she sought the help of a Russian Orthodox priest. Many physical and emotional maladies, she sensed, are really problems of the soul. Having no spiritual background herself, Lydia asked the local priest how a person—any person—could experience forgiveness. Could this sense of heaviness ever be lifted?

Forgiveness? the priest responded. Oh, yes. He had heard that was possible, but that was all he knew. "Here, take this," he offered finally, as he put in Lydia's hands the first Bible she'd ever seen. "Perhaps you can find something in this book about forgiveness."

Lydia started to read at the beginning, in the book of Genesis, hanging on through the patriarchs and the Psalms and the prophets until she came to the Gospels' account of Jesus. *It's here,* she realized. *The death and resurrection of Christ is the secret to being forgiven.*

That may not seem like a startling revelation to you or me—surely, there is more to this story. But for Lydia, who had no one to guide her, that understanding was revolutionary. It was like finding gold at the bottom of a pile of bricks. She began to do a few simple things based on her rudimentary faith—she read psalms to

*Indeed, it's true: because you and I are loved . . . we can come clean.*

her children at night and prayed ancient Russian Orthodox prayers for healing over them as they went to sleep. That was her expression of faith—of being forgiven.[8]

By the time my husband and I visited her (she'd met only a handful of people who identified themselves as Christians in her entire life), the children in her orphanage had improved so profoundly that doctors from other regions were coming to inquire about these novel remedies.

Whenever I think of the small miracle it truly is that we

can live, moment by moment, feeling received and forgiven by the Father, I think of Lydia. She saw the reality of that for the wonder it is. Do we?

This journey with the Lord literally brings light into the darkest corners of our hearts. The farther we travel, the more we see. Yet we do not shrink away in shame, fearing the rebuke of a stern father. Over time, the path home becomes more worn and familiar, the reception more assured. The Father has kept your plate warm at the party he is giving for you. Indeed, it's true: because you and I are loved . . . we can come clean.

Sometimes I remember how desperate my search for answers was at one point in my life—desperate enough to make Jungian psychology attractive. I still have more questions than answers. But God has done even better at what he hinted that day as I read Carl Jung while my children played outside. He's helped me find my heart. He's walked me into the embrace of his love. I think, perhaps, that's the essence of what I was looking for all along.

Life is anything but the tones of dull sepia these days. It has all the color and clash of a three-ring circus, and the music in the background is a wild hope I would not trade for anything.

# IDENTIFYING WITH THE PRODIGAL BROTHERS

*There are parts of me that have never heard the gospel.*

The story of the two prodigal brothers is the story we all live in various ways and at various times in our lives. It can provide you a much richer understanding of the aspects of your own heart that remain estranged and aloof—hesitant to come home to the embrace of the Father.

Find a secluded place and a small chunk of time so that you can read this story Jesus told (Luke 15:11–32). You are not reading it as an outsider looking on, however.

Try reading the story slowly twice, in present tense.[9] *You are the prodigal son who sees something out there that sounds and looks like life—and you want it badly enough to leave all you've been given.* See what God brings to mind as you picture leaving home . . . starving in a far country . . . returning in rags . . . letting the Father put his robe on you.

Then sit with this story a second time—only now, you are reading as the elder brother. *You've stayed home and done what you were supposed to do (or so you thought), and you're convinced that no one will ever throw you a party.* Can you feel the pride and indignation? What does God show you about the part of your own heart that somehow believes the Father will never really wrap his arms around you?

Take some time to journal about the feelings and thoughts that come to mind as you read. Where do you sense the Father's love?

Are you able to let yourself come home? What would that look like for you? What would that mean in your own life?

# Chapter 5

# GROWING UP TOGETHER

## RELATIONSHIPS WHERE YOU CAN KNOW . . . AND BE KNOWN

> *Sometimes you are the pigeon—*
> *and sometimes you are the statue.*
> —OLD COUNTRY PROVERB

> *Do nothing from selfishness or empty conceit,*
> *but with humility of mind regard one*
> *another as more important than yourselves.*
> —PHILIPPIANS 2:3

*When Sam's girls were small, his job often kept him away* from home, traveling to various sales meetings. What he remembers most from those years were the first moments when he'd return. Three sets of outstretched, little-girl arms greeted him as he walked through the door, thrilled Daddy was home.

But daughters grow up, as daughters do—and soon, they have children of their own. One evening when the whole family had gathered for a meal, Sam pushed back his plate and between mouthfuls of strawberry pie, he floated what seemed like an innocent question. "What was it like for you girls growing up, when I traveled so much?" he asked, thinking it might be good to review a little family history.

His daughters began to talk, one by one, and the story behind the story poured out. Sam quietly put down his fork and sat back in his chair. For the first time he grasped the impact of his absences. The loneliness they felt. How much they missed having a dad around. The responsibility of keeping life together for their mother. With a few tears and a bit of anger, the story came out piece by piece as if it had been stored in a safe-deposit box for just such a moment.

Sam could have buttoned up this conversation and moved on to a fresh topic, but he let his daughters talk. He asked the kind of questions that made him feel uncomfortable. He is such a man of courage. And then Sam took a deep breath and said, "I'm so sorry I didn't realize what was happening in your life when I was gone. I think I was too preoccupied to hear you—and I was wrong not to ask sooner."

Sam would say that this conversation was a turning point in his life—especially in his relationship with his daughters. It was like some kind of fog lifted. When he thinks of the friendships that have now emerged with his daughters and their husbands, he knows a good portion has come from the simple humility of being able to say, *I was wrong. And I am sorry.*

## WHAT WE FEAR

On one level, my friend's admission of guilt sounds like the most obvious thing in the world to say. Of course, he was sorry he was gone so much. But you can choke on words like these when you are speaking them to someone who really matters to you. To admit you're wrong—to own your impact on another person—can feel like you've just given them permission to write you off. Forever. That's why only the strong can be vulnerable.

Have you ever been struck by the small miracle it is that Christ makes you strong enough to bear the humility of being wrong—that in him, you can weather the gaze of someone you love who feels you've failed him or her miserably? That is no easy thing. Some people never get there. But this kind of humility brings with it enormous freedom—all kinds of possibilities in being loved and loving others well. It is a gold mine, relationally.

I think the apostle Paul had this in mind when he prayed that we would be "strengthened with power . . . in the inner man" so that we could know the love of Christ in all its length and breadth and depth (Eph. 3:16–19). Paul wanted us to take a bath in the love of Jesus, so to speak—to let his love coat our vulnerabilities so we can risk really letting people in. The love of Christ can carry us past the fear of rejection.

The gospel, as good as it is, will mean little to us unless it gets pulled into our personal relationships and the way we hide from each other. I think with gratitude on that season of my life in which I was disillusioned with my faith and intrigued by Jungian thought. Where would I have been without a good friend who looked into my mess and saw how much I was struggling?

> *The love of Christ can carry us past the fear of rejection.*

She pulled me aside one day and said a few words that I know weren't easy for her to say. "I'm concerned about you, Paula," she began. "I think you are barking up the wrong tree. Where is Christ in all your searching? What is the restlessness about?"

She kind of rained on my parade. I was embarrassed that she saw my discontent and wanted to pull the plug on enlightenment. But I also realized her words were those of a friend, concerned for the direction my struggle was taking me.

Where else but in the body of Christ can we find people who are willing to risk their relationships with us in order to tell us the truth?

## THE MARK OF MATURITY

When I'm struggling to lay hold of honesty and humility in a relationship, I sometimes have flashbacks of my son at two years old, in that stage of orneriness that makes you want to hire a nanny. Caught in some flagrant act of willfulness, Brady would reap his just recompense. I'd put him on my lap and comfort him through his tears, trying to instill the art of confession.

"Now, Brady, you need to say you're sorry," I'd tell him, hoping to prompt an ounce or two of contrition.

Without skipping a beat, Brady would stick out his lip and insist, "I am *not* sorry!" And I'd think, *Well, we've got a ways to go here.* Apparently, remorse is something of a learned response.

When you think about it, remorse and humility are staples in the Christian faith. Each week, in the church my husband and I attend, we get on our knees to silently confess our sins. And then the congregation stands up to sing. Those are the two basic movements of the soul—we admit we continually fall short, and we celebrate the scandal of God's grace. We receive his forgiveness.

Or think of the sacrament of Communion. You come forward or gather around a table with others—empty hands outstretched. The truth about you is spoken in public. *The body and blood of Christ, given for you.* Your need is spelled out—in fact, it's almost trumpeted.

We reenact this drama that puts our inadequacy and our sin in center stage before God and *with each other*, claiming together the mercy of God through his cross. If we're paying attention, the jig is up. There's no need to posture and pretend anymore. If we were truly shining stars and perfect people, we would not be gathered around this table. The sacrifice of Christ would not be necessary.

The body of Christ may be the only group you've ever

belonged to where your deficiency—not your talents or your expertise—is what qualifies you for membership.

You can understand, then, how strange it feels to witness Christians who are locked in a struggle with each other—and a moment comes when the simple admission of guilt would clear some of the air. Even the acknowledgment "I've caused you pain, and I'm sorry" would help. Isn't it tragic when we let the silence reign . . . and dig deeper into our fortified position?

The truth is that if we are alive and breathing and still on this fallen planet, then, no matter how justified we feel, we are at fault somewhere in the picture. Somehow we missed something. And our faith is what most enables us to name it and claim it.

The measure of our maturity is not how together we appear—but rather, the small moments when we are able to suffer the indignity of having our flaws and inadequacies exposed to someone we love. It's a peculiar grace, indeed.

Quite literally, the humility of owning our stuff breaks open the hard and frozen places in a close relationship—and God pours in the oil of his grace so that something new can happen.

Thank God, something new can happen.

## TO RISK BEING KNOWN

Indeed, more is possible in relationships because of Christ. What we actually experience with each other, though, is directly proportional to the risks we are prepared to take. In other words, you don't get the chance to exhale—to find real places of safety and support in relationships—without taking a number of deep breaths. That sucking-in-air sensation is the way courage feels.

It takes a deep breath to put yourself out there in a friendship, doesn't it? Even in a marriage we can live as virtual strangers, unknown at any true depth.

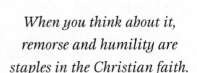

*When you think about it, remorse and humility are staples in the Christian faith.*

Sometimes when I speak to women's groups, I ask a simple question. "When was the last time someone leaned across a table and said, 'So . . . how are *you* doing . . . I mean really?'" I see such longing on so many faces. Many of us lack anyone who knows us very well. Sometimes, though, the people who would ask a deeply personal question can't get past the parlor of our lives to ever see us with our hair down. *We have not let ourselves be known.*

I admit, though—that's no easy task. To share the truth of who we are feels like a risk because, indeed, it "may not gain us anything, we're afraid, but an uneasy silence and a fishy stare."[1] Or as Brennan Manning states in his own lively way:

Whom can I level with? To whom can I bare my soul? Whom dare I tell that I am benevolent and malevolent, chaste and randy, compassionate and vindictive, selfless and selfish, that beneath my brave words lives a frightened child . . . that I have blackened a friend's character, betrayed a trust, violated a confidence, that I am tolerant and thoughtful, a bigot and a blowhard, and that I really hate okra?[2]

There is always a risk in relationship—but it's a risk God means for us to take. I remember discussing this need with Chris, the woman who was addicted to prescription pain medication. She was determined to beat her problem on her own. She didn't want anyone to see her weakness.

"Then the body of Christ is useless to you," I offered in response. "You are missing the best part. Not everyone can handle where your life is. But God will give you a few trusted folks who will share your battle. You don't have to spend your life in hiding."

The love of Christ can heal us, truly. Yet most often, the love of Christ heals us *through each other*, as our shame is known. Perhaps that's why James includes this startling prescription for living the good life: "Confess your sins to each other and pray for each other so that you may be healed" (5:16 NIV).

> *What we actually experience with each other, though, is directly proportional to the risks we are prepared to take.*

That simple practice of humility is surprisingly powerful. Your need is out in the open, spoken in the presence of others—real, flesh-and-blood people who, by the modest act of hearing and praying, mirror the actual love and acceptance of God.

I sometimes think that these little moments strung together

are really the primary way our souls are shaped. These moments are vastly underrated. It's like a story a friend recently shared with me. She's the quintessential mother who taught her four children to read—the kind of cookie-baking nurturer the rest of us wish we were. Only my friend has one daughter whose navel piercing and bad grades and rebellious attitude have nearly undone her. She is running out of patience. Every tactic she takes with her daughter seems to fail—it's so embarrassing.

So my friend shared with a few people (none of whom had a difficult child) how at her wit's end, she felt. She asked, simply, if they would pray for her.

> *I sometimes think that these little moments strung together are really the primary way our souls are shaped.*

We were talking later about how, strangely enough, this has helped. "How is it," she mused out loud, "that talking about how impossible I find it to love my daughter these days and then letting someone pray for me makes a difference? I don't understand, but in the oddest way, I've been more patient ever since."

We both shake our heads in wonder, really, at the way God applies such mysterious grace to the wounds of our souls *through each other.*

How hard do you find it to say to someone, "I'm struggling with this . . ." or "I feel like such a failure at that . . . Would you pray for me?" You don't want to miss what is available to you by staying glued to your mask. You want the body of Christ to be all God means for it to be in your life.

## HOW WE GROW UP

Strolling through a small country store, I stumbled on a painted sign that summarized the plainest truth about relationships I've seen in one sentence.

*Sometimes you are the pigeon—*
*and sometimes you are the statue.*

Can it be said any more succinctly? If we want our lives uncluttered and free of drama, then we need to find a hillside and camp out alone. Real relationships are messy. They inevitably bring a share of pigeon droppings. Sometimes you are the one who feels dumped on—and other times, you're the pigeon doing the dumping, and someone else, literally, feels the impact.

There are sophisticated ways of saying this, of course. The best one is that we are all both victims and agents. To live together as fallen people, on the far side of Eden, means that we hurt each other, and we are hurt by each other—often in nearly equal measure. No one's hands are clean. Letting that reality touch you deeply will bring something wonderful—it's what the Bible calls "humility of mind." Here is the way the apostle Paul writes about it:

Do nothing from selfishness or empty conceit, but with
humility of mind regard one another as more important
than yourselves; do not merely look out for your own personal interests, but also for the interests of others. (Phil.
2:3–4)

A dose of humility goes a long way in a friendship or a
marriage. It's the hidden ticket to nearly everything we call
*real* in a relationship.

Henri Nouwen once said that true Christian community
is not like just having a circle of friends—because true community always includes someone we don't like. She grates on
our nerves. She reminds me of my weakness. I would not
pick her for a friend, really, and yet, *voila!* God has put her
in my life. That is the gift, actually. In a context of grace, I am
reminded of my own neediness and failure, and thereby,
humility opens me to receive from God as he touches my life
through other people.

Experiencing the grace of Christ makes true relationship
with each other possible. But make no mistake. The mess
and the grace are present with each other at the same time,
perhaps more than we bargained for. There will be moments that call for painful apology and others that look like
scary confrontation. We won't be in any relationship long
before our selfishness starts to show—or real sacrifice is
called for.

If we ever grow up, we will have to grow up together.

## WHAT WE TASTE TOGETHER

One scene in John's Gospel account is a window into how God makes us able to live boldly the life he has for us. It's a picture of what it means to experience Christ *with each other* so that our lives are actually transformed.

John devotes more space to this story than to any other story. In fact, the details in John 21 are so specific you can practically taste the fish being cooked by the Sea of Galilee.

The central character is Peter (who often manages to be the central character). The storyline is his failure—his huge, honking, glaring denial that he ever knew this man, Jesus, who was his Savior. Peter has returned to his day job as a fisherman. He has failed as a follower of Jesus—but at least, perhaps, he can still catch a few fish. Surely that much he can do.

The resurrected Christ appears by the Sea of Galilee after Peter has, once again, fished all night and caught nothing. Jesus steps right into the middle of all Peter's failure and shame. But this scene takes place with Peter *among his closest friends*. They know what Peter's done. They listen in on this conversation between Jesus and Peter, missing not a word.

Three times Jesus asks Peter if he loves him. Three times Peter insists that he does. And each time, Christ invites Peter to take that love and shepherd his sheep.

Wait a minute. Peter, who denied Christ when he most needed him, is going to be a shepherd of the early church? Who would believe that Christ would be so generous, so utterly gracious as to offer Peter his original place in the scheme of things? I wonder if Peter's friends choked on their fish as they watched.

When I consider the man Peter became and his role in the early church, I suspect that his power and boldness are directly connected to this scene. Peter does become the rock Christ said he would be. He is utterly fearless—grateful, even, that his witness is bold enough to mark him by the authorities as a threat. Walking more than three thousand miles in his lifetime to share the gospel, Peter's influence transformed Asia Minor into the Christian corner of the Roman Empire.

Something life changing happened for Peter among his friends. Perhaps his boldness is at least partially the result of having little else to hide. Peter experienced grace not unlike the way you and I must—as our failure and shame become known, in some small way, in the company of others who name his name and believe Christ is actually present in our midst.

The expression of transforming fellowship I know personally takes place, not by the Sea of Galilee but under a North Carolina canopy of pine trees on various Sunday evenings. It's a collection of six couples who came together, innocently enough, in the beginning—when we still thought we had life by the tail. There were no glaring problems, no debilitating illnesses. We just met to share a portion of Scripture—to share our lives. What could be simpler?

Fifteen years have come and gone now. A lot has changed. We've weathered cancer treatments and struggling ministries, business reversals and children determined to sow their oats. Some evenings we show up hoping no one will ask what's happening in our lives—because even though they know, we'd rather not elaborate. It's better to simply pray about the obvious. Slowly, through the years, this fellowship has become its own kind of womb, nurturing this Christ-life within us—this Christ-life being poured out on many others.

There is a great gift in knowing people too well to successfully hide your flaws. Surely Peter experienced this. The polish wears off rather quickly when Jesus is present. Our group under the pine trees has been together a long time—long enough to disappoint each other occasionally. Yet we have chosen to hang together and let grace work its magic. In the oddest sort of way, the failure of our humanness makes the fellowship richer.

*Something life changing happened for Peter among his friends. Perhaps his boldness is at least partially the result of having little else to hide.*

Perhaps nowhere in our journey of following Christ, past the rubble of broken dreams, do we stumble on any better gift—the sweet grace of being on that path with other folks. It's true—we are not what we will one day be. Yet God is generous. We taste his mercy even now through the forgiveness and encouragement we experience together. He gives us a few hands to hold along the way.

# TELLING YOUR STORY

*What we hunger for perhaps more than anything else is to be known in our full humanness, and yet that is often just what we fear more than anything else.*
—FREDERICK BUECHNER

Each of us has a story. It's a tale that includes the best of times—and probably, some painful experiences as well. It's all part of the way God is shaping our lives for his glory and purposes.

We can't discover our own story alone, really. Pieces of understanding about how God is at work in your life come only as you share your story in the presence of others. It's a mysterious and powerful experience in which there is always more to be learned.

Simply invite two or three friends who also see their lives as a journey with Christ that's going somewhere . . . and mark off an entire morning or afternoon. Turn off the phone. Close the door and put on a big pot of coffee or tea.

Ask each of your friends to come prepared with a few notes or a timeline that marks the peak shaping experiences and low points in their lives—their own particular mix of the good, the bad, and the ugly. You are thinking through your life in broad brushstrokes of important events and influences, not the fine points and details ("I left home on September 4, 1985 . . . ").

Divide the time allotted by the number of participants, and hand a watch to the woman who will agree to gently watch the time. (Often when you are telling your story, time disappears.) Then let each woman share her story, noting what is significant to her.

Restrict your comments on each other's stories to two things: how you see God at work in another woman's life and what you heard that touches you deeply in some way. Resist the urge to offer advice or counsel. Now is a time to listen and take in. Most people have never experienced any-one who just listened to them.

At the beginning of the time together, take a few moments to ask God to lead you . . . and then at the end, spend a while thanking God for what you've experienced or have come to understand about yourself or each other.

*Chapter 6*

# COMING IN SECOND

## RESTING IN THE SHADE OF
## THE SOVEREIGNTY OF GOD

*We make ourselves sane when we fire ourselves*
*as the director of the movie of our lives*
*and turn the power over to Him.*
—BEN STEIN

*I know that you can do all things;*
*no plan of yours can be thwarted.*
—JOB 42:2 NIV

*I secretly believe that I'm the queen of second-guessing,* though I know many women who would vie for the title. To be honest, there are a slew of moments in life that literally beg to be second-guessed. Some decisions you wish you could undo. You can be dying in a pool of regret before you even know what happened to you.

One of my clearer memories of this occurred the first morning I awoke in North Carolina. For years I had quietly pined to move back east where I grew up. Though I loved the people in Oklahoma, the shopping in Texas, and the blue sky of Colorado—I nursed a secret longing to see our moving van head *the other way*. Coming home would not be moonlight and magnolias, I knew, though I did have visions of seeing our children catch lightning bugs in jars on warm summer nights. I had visions of many things. But childhood memories rarely reincarnate into adult dreams. Thomas Wolfe was right: you can't go home again.

Let it be noted, though, that I tried. After many years of living out west, an amazing door opened for us to pack up our lives and return to the land of sweet tea and grits. The moving van was finally heading east.

So there I was, waking up that first morning in our newly purchased home in North Carolina. Cool sheets, recently unpacked, covered my tired body. The air was heavy with humidity (Southerners actually claim that helps you sleep). The windows were flung wide open; I wanted to be totally immersed in the sound of songbirds and crickets. I was lying there on my back, arms folded across my grateful chest, thanking Jesus profusely for a miracle I never thought would happen—moving home.

*One of life's little ironies is that some of our hardest times are when our dreams actually do come true.*

And then I heard it. All sound became one, and it wasn't a bird. It was a plane roaring over those pine trees. Another followed in close succession, leaving a trail of pepper dust across the Carolina blue sky. I know this for a fact—for in the words of the classic Christmas poem, I sprang from my bed to see what was the matter.

"Oh, dear gussie." That's all I could say, over and over, as I stared out the window, feeling sick. *Dear gussie.* (That translates to *great days* or *holy smokes* or various expressions in other parts of the country.) *We have bought a home in an American Airlines flight pattern.*

What comes next in this story is fairly predictable. The regrets lined up like heavy freight planes being cleared for landing. The season of second-guessing came upon me with a vengeance. One of life's little ironies is that some of our hardest times are when our dreams actually do come true.

I realize there are a lot worse temptations to second-guess yourself than the purchase of a home (in which I still live and slowly grew to love). Marriage, for example, can be a tale of waking up to another person's flaws and foibles, little surprises on the other side of the altar that can make you wonder what you signed on for. Women often reach points in their journey where they question earlier decisions. And it's true—we all make some poor and even sinful choices from which we learn some tough lessons the hard way.

But most looking back is like my friend reading all her Christmas letters, tales filled with yuletide warmth and children's triumphs, and wondering why she's still single at forty. *Where did I miss the boat?* Or regret takes the shape of *if only.* If only I'd gone to a different college . . . if only I hadn't lost my job at such a vulnerable moment. If only, if only, if only. *If only* can be a heavy sandbag to carry through life.

As I stared out the window that morning at the planes roaring above our home, the litany of regret in my head was harder to unpack than the cardboard boxes at my feet. For months to come, I wondered how we missed the glaringly obvious—especially since this was not an impulsive or prayerless decision. I grilled my motives for wanting to move in the first place. It would have been safer to stay put. I lived in a world that is familiar to many women—the land of coulda . . . shoulda . . . woulda.

And that's no place to set up camp.

## THE MYTH OF THE YELLOW BRICK ROAD

Has your story taken a few turns that have caught you by surprise? Or do you ever look back and wish your life was on movable rollers so you could rearrange the pieces? This time, you'd get it *right*.

I have talked to enough women now to know that I am in good company. Here are a couple of things that happen in a woman's heart if she gets stuck looking in the rearview mirror.

### THE SEARCH FOR CERTAINTY
Hidden behind most of our regrets is the myth of the guaranteed right choice—as though if we'd only done it right, the

path would have been smooth. There is a yellow brick road, we think, and our job from birth is to find it.

God surely holds the keys to this certain path that we desperately need to find. And when we get there, it should feel like tiptoeing through the tulips—some kind of emotional proof we are on target. The Bible never paints our lives this way, though. If you read the fine print, you notice that guarantees and certainty apply only to the life to come. The here and now is seen through a glass darkly.

The search for guarantees can leave you cautious and tentative about nearly everything—always fearful that your next choice will prove (yet again) to be some kind of mistake you regret. It mutates into the bad habit of worry, a crazy virus if there ever was one, because worry appears to ward off the next set of bad things happening. And so we keep doing it. But really, it just makes you go through life like Steve Martin's character in *Father of the Bride*, gripping the roller coaster with white knuckles while everyone else enjoys the ride.

I find my own perspective changes when I can let the present be something God is shaping for a future I cannot see— *and that something is good* because God is good. That may sound simple, but it's truer than thinking I can find the yellow brick road if I'm smart enough. Even in darker moments when I wonder if I have indeed missed God through my own hardheadedness (a genuine possibility), I am comforted by remembering that I belong to Christ—and I cannot, then, be truly lost again. It helps me to stop looking so hard for the certain path and lean the weight of my life on the God who owns them all.

## PRACTICAL ATHEISM

It's hard to be a Christian who lives like an atheist, but that's where this all ends up. Living in regret and second-guessing is the door to feeling really alone—because, remember, if you hadn't screwed things up somehow, you could have made a veritable daisy chain out of that bed of flowers you should, by now, have found.

But since you did not look up and see the planes overhead, so to speak—or perhaps you got badly hurt by someone you trusted—then there is nothing left but to patrol the edges of your life with renewed vigilance. Alone. God has left you with a list of things to accomplish, and like a good employer he will check in at five o'clock to see what you got done. I'm only being mildly facetious because this is how many of us live. *As though it all depends on us.*

I try to remind myself how sad it is to live like an atheist with the gospel sitting at my fingertips. But if you add the regrets of the past to your fears of the future, you will end up paralyzed in the present. And feeling very alone. Combining *if I had only* with *what if this-or-that happens down the road* is one heavy ball of angst. This is, actually, the textbook anxiety that drives good people into addictions like alcoholism— and even without the alcohol, it's no way to live.

The truth is that if it all depends on us, we are in worse trouble than we think.

## A DIFFERENT WAY TO LIVE

I have a theory that's been formed in moments of personal reflection on this topic. No matter what your spiritual background, if you make the journey of life in Christ well, I believe you will eventually come face-to-face with the sovereignty of God.

Though conceptually quite sophisticated, it could be stated something like this:

> The God who spoke the worlds into existence and keeps the stars in place is the God who knows you like no one will ever know you. He has always loved you. He will love you to the end. His purposes for you are so set in place that you can rest every minute of your journey in the cool shade of his merciful sovereignty over your life.

The theme of God's sovereignty is woven through Scripture like a golden thread that runs from beginning to end. No one puts it more succinctly, though, than the writer of Proverbs:

> The mind of man plans his way,
> But the LORD directs his steps. (16:9)

We can plan all we want. We can map out our five-year goals and make a dozen to-do lists a day. But God orders our steps. He opens and closes the doors that matter. He is really God—which is to say that he is *really God.*

I think of the sovereignty of God in my own life as the quiet surrender to his *authority*—meaning that I acknowledge him as the *Author* of my story.[1] It's not that there aren't choices that need to be weighed out prayerfully. But my vision is limited. And I'm not in control of all the variables. So it helps to acknowledge God in his greatness—the actual Author of my story. He is writing a tale of redemption through our lives in which every act of the drama is part of a bigger story than we can see.

I want to rest in the sovereignty of God in such a way that it actually shapes my heart. Or as Don Miller, author of *Blue Like Jazz*, expresses in starkly concrete terms:

> I actually need to believe there is something bigger than me, and I need for there to be something bigger than me . . . I need to come second to someone who has everything figured out.[2]

*I need to come second to someone who has everything figured out.* I can feel myself exhale in relief even as I write the words. For as much as I fight to be in control, I need to know when I wake up and hear the planes roaring past that God knew what we didn't. God was not caught by surprise, even though I was. If I let myself take comfort where comfort is due, then I begin to anticipate a larger purpose in being in this house and this place than enduring irritating noise.

There is a world of comfort in the sovereignty of God—like the shade of a huge oak tree you can lean your tired soul upon. Perhaps this is why Paul begins his most complete treatise on what it means to be a Christian with a word that lifts you right out of time and places your life in God's larger story:

> Blessed be the God and Father of our Lord Jesus Christ, who
> . . . chose us in Him before the foundation of the world, that
> we would be holy and blameless before Him. (Eph. 1:3–4)

That verse and dozens like it are meant to slide you through a time warp into realizing that, in some amazing way, you actually have a life in God that preexists you—where every piece of the drama serves a good and larger purpose riddled with the light of his glory. We only get a peek behind the curtain from time to time, and that can be frustrating. But the whole universe whispers the same refrain—that when the curtain finally parts and we *see*, what we see will take our breath away.

## WHAT CAN CHANGE FOR US

I should admit, though, that the phrase *the sovereignty of God* has been terribly abused in certain quarters. Some awful tragedy strikes, and supposedly you can color over every doubt and painful grief in a placid acceptance of God's larger purposes—like a brighter shade of lipstick would cover everything.

Sometimes we say, "God is sovereign" as though it was a yellow sticky note big enough to cover a poor human choice that some poor human needs to admit and take responsibility for. God is not a cosmic rug we get to sweep our junk under. There is no substitute for the simple and powerful words, *I did this, and I'm sorry.*

With that said, though, it will help to explore how living in the shade of God's ultimate power and authority puts something solid beneath our feet. I think David summarizes best the perspective we can gain as he writes:

> From the end of the earth I call to You, when my heart is faint;
>> Lead me to the rock that is higher than I. (Ps. 61:2)

God wants to lift us above the muddle of our situations so we can see from a higher plane—even though our sight is only a glimpse. God's heart is to bring us to a rock that is higher than we are because from there, life looks different.

## HOW WE INTERPRET OUR STORY

Of all the ways the sovereignty of God affects how we see life, how we interpret our story is perhaps the most foundational. Often, the very things we call meaningless detours in our journey turn out to be the path we were supposed to be traveling. We have come home—but by a road we would not have known to choose.

I think of a conversation with a talented woman named Sylvia, who sees her life as something of a failure. Her labeling felt unusual to me, since it was clear that the woman I was talking to was both capable and accomplished.

"You don't understand," she corrected me with a note of exasperation. "I am midway through my thirties and just now discovering something I want to pursue. I feel way behind my friends."

As she shared her story, she described how she had given five years of her twenties to setting up adoption services in China, which she loved doing. When she returned home, though, it seemed as if she had lost her way—or so she felt. And of course, it was all her fault.

"There's no man in my life," she continued. "No golden door has opened to the great career. I've had four dead-end jobs in five years. It's taken all this time for me to find a path I really want to pursue. I feel like such a failure."

I sensed as we talked just how shaken her confidence really was—and how distant God seemed to her. "How are you going to look at what you're calling 'the wasted years'? I mean, where has God been in all that?" I asked.

God had mostly been waiting for her to get her act together, she replied, and we both laughed.

"But God could have shown you what you needed to see a month after you left China, and he didn't," I reminded her. "How are you going to let that mean something in your life?"

This is truly the crucial question for each of us. How am I going to allow the detours and the lost years and the mistakes to take their proper place in a life that is, somehow, being orchestrated by a God who loves me? Can I let myself

accept that I am living a directed life even when I feel that I am
floundering?

The small miracle is that if the merciful sovereignty of God
is real, then we are freed from the tyranny of having to measure
every memory in terms of failure or success. It's such a relief to
lay down that crazy measuring stick.

Perhaps my friend's struggle to find her way is not a pile of
wasted years in the real scheme of things. I think that is much
closer to the truth. I suspect she will come to see that those years
contained tiny seeds that blossomed in ways she can hardly imagine now. There is an old expression that comforts because it's just so true: *God never wastes an experience on us.* If we have given ourselves to him in any true measure, we find it all serves. All of it.

> *How am I going to allow the detours and the lost years and the mistakes to take their proper place in a life that is, somehow, being orchestrated by a God who loves me?*

So discovering the shade of God's sovereignty is no small
matter. It literally changes the lens through which you see your
life—this story God is writing that is bigger than you can even
think to dream.

# THE LARGER STORY GOD IS WRITING

*You meant evil against me, but God meant it for good in order to bring about this present result, to preserve many people alive.*
—GENESIS 50:20

Perhaps the story in the Bible that most invites us to take shade in the sovereignty of God is the Old Testament story of Joseph. Do you remember how boldly young Joseph told his brothers about his dream that, one day, he would be the guy in charge? And indeed, he became second only to Pharaoh, able to use his position and power to provide for his brothers who had disowned him.

In between, though, Joseph was sold into slavery, framed by a seductive woman, and spent thirteen years in prison. I wonder if Joseph could have even imagined how difficult the road would be between his original dream . . . and God's fulfillment.

Joseph didn't just waste away in prison, though. He came to realize some very deep things about God's purposes in his life. He reveals what he learned in the names he gave his sons:

*Manasseh*, which means, "God has made me forget all my trouble and all my father's household."

*Ephraim,* which means, "God has made me fruitful in the land of my affliction."

> Part of the reason that Joseph could forgive his brothers was that he saw God's greater purposes playing out in the big picture of his life.
>
> "You meant evil against me," Joseph said, "but God meant it for good *in order to bring about this present result, to preserve many people alive*" (Gen. 50:20; emphasis added).
>
> I often return to Joseph's life when I need to be reminded that God is writing a larger story than the one I can see.

## WHO HOLDS THE POWER OVER US

It's easy to look through the rearview mirror and see the roads not taken—or how choices others made affected our lives. God must be bigger than our own mistakes. And he must be sovereign over the choices others make—the ones that also touch our lives. A woman who feels she's at the mercy of others never really sees the power of God—or her own personal power to make choices.

Lily was a woman in the throes of a broken engagement to a guy named Scott. She so wanted to marry this man. They dated a few years and talked about the future they were planning together. Out of the blue, though, her mother was killed in a car accident and Lily was washed out to sea with the grief of losing her. Sudden death can really stun those who are left behind—and for a whole year, Lily could only put one foot in front of the other and survive. Scott hung in there, supporting her as best he could. But their relationship was put on hold.

When Lily was ready to move forward, Scott found that he wasn't. The feelings he put on a back burner had now grown cold. He finally had to say the words no one wants to hear: "I'm sorry, but my heart is no longer in this."

You can imagine how upset Lily was. She'd lost the two people in the world she most loved. She replayed the story a thousand times in her mind. If only her mother hadn't died. If only she could have been more available to a relationship when Scott was. If Scott had been just a bit more mature and understanding. If only. Who among us has not heard that painful, broken record play in the lonely corners of our minds?

It would be naive to suggest that regret and second-guessing can be avoided when we are hit with a loss so dear—as if there were a slick detour around that big pothole. Our hearts need to process what has happened. But I do suggest that it is tragic to get stuck there. Lily is not a victim. And you and I are not at the whim of another person's choices and affections.

The sovereignty of God releases us from this place where we beat ourselves up for the response we could not give—or the feelings we could not produce. "God is greater than our heart" (1 John 3:20).

But God is also able to direct the affections and choices of anyone who touches our lives. "The king's heart is like channels of water in the hand of the LORD; He turns it wherever He wishes" (Prov. 21:1). If someone's heart changes, then I have to (eventually) conclude God has allowed that shift, for reasons beyond my ability to see. Trusting that is often the first step to a new and hopeful anticipation of what God might bring in its place.

## WHAT MIGHT BE SIMPLY IS NOT

Years ago, I came upon the words of Jim Elliot, a missionary killed by Auca Indians in Ecuador to whom he brought the gospel. His death opened the door to the conversion of this remote jungle tribe. In a letter to his wife before his death, he wrote about the experiences they could have enjoyed together—the time they might have spent in each other's company.[3] I have returned to his words many times when I feel the loss of something I had anticipated but which fails to happen—all the what-could-have-beens of life. Elliott writes:

> What is, is actual—what might be *simply is not*, and I must not therefore query God as though he robbed me—of things that are not . . . [the] things that *are* belong to us, and they are good, God-given and enriched.[4]

There is a quiet release in my spirit (though it can be slow in coming) when I realize that often, my dreams really are not God's dreams. What does not happen was not meant to take place. My failure—or someone else's failure—didn't catch God by surprise, like it slipped under the wire when he wasn't looking. In the words of Job as he spoke to God, "I know that you can do all things; no plan of yours can be thwarted" (Job 42:2 NIV).

## THE BIG PICTURE

More than anything else, a grasp of the merciful sovereignty of God allows you to live as a woman who smiles at the future and who accepts her past. There is a bigger drama taking place than you can see through the keyhole now.

Perhaps you had to experience something on the darker side of life to really appreciate the blazing light of Jesus. Maybe you could never offer true comfort to hurting people if you had not tasted pain so bitter it took your breath away. Perhaps there were flaws in your husband you were meant to miss because there is something more important being worked into both of your hearts than an easy relationship.

I'm sure that, had I not lived on the hot plains of Oklahoma, I would have missed knowing people so genuine they said exactly what they thought. Yet at the time, I used to wake up most mornings wondering how on earth we had come there to broil under that sun.

The house in North Carolina with more planes than birds overhead turned out to be a stone's throw from the only high school in the eastern half of the state where two hours a day of aeronautics were offered in the curriculum. Our son now flies one of those same commercial jets, leaving pepper trails across other skies.

I would not for a moment imply that all stories come out neatly packaged. Lots of loose strings in our lives get tied into happier endings past any horizon we can see. God is great, and God is good as the child's prayer says—but sometimes his greatness and his goodness come together much farther down the road than we would hope.

C. S. Lewis claims that the problem is one of *transposition*, which is an interesting word he explained this way. Lewis says that the sovereignty and goodness of God is like a symphony that fills the largest concert hall with the most beautiful music imaginable. Only you and I are not in that room. Rather, we are listening to the music through a grainy radio at the kitchen table, trying to follow the melody through the static.[5] That image keeps me sane when I find myself trying to catch, once again, the faint notes of the song God is playing in my life.

## GOD IS DOING SOMETHING MORE

Let me invite you to step out of your culture and time for a moment—and enter a true story that emerged in 1992 as the former Soviet Union began to undo seventy years of atheism. Whenever you want to be reminded that God is doing something more in your life than you will live to see, think of this Russian grandmother.[6]

The setting is the countryside of St. Petersburg on a day cold enough to keep everyone but the crows inside. A startling permission has been handed down from local officials—an opportunity too good to wait for better weather. The large warehouse outside town filled floor to ceiling with thousands of Russian Bibles, confiscated during Stalin's regime, is being unlocked for the first time in decades. At last, these Bibles can be redistributed by Christians to families who have not seen a Bible in years.

It's like a big party—for everyone except Ivan, a young Russian man who agreed to load trucks with these strange books. He is one of many others who have grown up to see his country in shambles, Lenin's statue ground to dust. There is no future for him, no job, and he is bitter and alone. This day represents a paycheck to him and nothing more.

About an hour into the morning, one of the Christians loading trucks looks over and notices that Ivan is sitting on the curb with a well-worn Bible in his hands. He is weeping.

The cause of his tears is this. Out of literally thousands of Bibles, the first one that Ivan lays his hand on is his own grandmother's.[7] She lived with his family many years, tolerated as the *babushka* but shunned by Ivan's father because she did not welcome the brave new world of Lenin. She paid a steep price for holding on to her faith. Ivan's family thought of her as an old fool who still believed in God and the fairy tales in the Bible.

Ivan's tears are the first drops from his cold heart starting to melt. Maybe there is a God in heaven who knows him and who heard his grandmother's prayers and who answered years and years later in a moment no human could engineer. What are the chances that of all the books his hands might touch, the first one was his own grandmother's? Ivan was speechless.

I believe there are more parallels between our lives—and this *babushka's*—than we might think. I suspect she was tempted to consider her life a failure. I bet she wondered on occasion if God had forgotten her or if she was being punished for some secret sin. I think there must have been moments when God whispered in her ear the gentle hope that he would win the day. Even in her own family, he would win the day.

I like to think of taking my place right beside her under the cool shade of the merciful sovereignty of God.

# LETTING GO OF YOUR REGRETS

*For the LORD God is a sun and shield;*
*The LORD gives grace and glory;*
*No good thing does He withhold*
*from those who walk uprightly.*
—PSALM 84:11

If your past holds a few things you find difficult to leave in the past, you may find this exercise helpful.

Find a quiet place where you can be alone for a brief time without being interrupted. Begin, simply, by thanking God that he has been present at every moment in your life. Thank him that nothing has taken him by surprise and that everything in your life has meaning and purpose.

Ask God to bring to mind the experiences and memories that are marked by regrets you had some choice about. *If only I had . . . or If only I hadn't . . .*

Make a list of those regrets. What is painful about the memories? What do you wish could have been different? What do you think a different choice would have meant in your life?

Then take a few minutes and simply talk with God about how you feel concerning each regret you have listed. Express to him your hope that these choices are part of his larger purposes in your life. Ask him to redeem what seems lost to you—and ask him to restore.

And finally, the most important part: as an act of leaving this regret with God, tear up the list. It may help to burn the pieces in a safe place or toss them in a moving stream of water. Before the day is done, share with one person what you have chosen to let go.

If your mind picks up an old regret, like fingering a rosary bead, then intentionally return to this place in your memory where you watched a piece of paper go up in flames or float down the creek.

*Chapter 7*

# THE EMPATHY OF JESUS

WHEN YOU NO LONGER
WONDER IF GOD CARES

*Oh, to see my name
Written in the wounds,
For your suffering I am free
Death is crushed to death;
Life is mine to live
Won through your selfless love.
This the power of the cross,
Son of God—slain for us.
What a love! What a cost!
We stand forgiven at the cross.*[1]
—KEITH GETTY

*The LORD of hosts is with us;
The God of Jacob is our stronghold.*
—PSALM 46:7

*In the drizzling rain that followed a summer evening's storm,*
a woman named Stella stopped to help a stranded motorist on
the edge of town. Even now, she doesn't consider her actions
particularly heroic. She's just not a drive-on-by sort of person.

Stella simply pulled off the side of the road and got out of her car, wading through a few puddles in her sandals to offer assistance. As she did, an intoxicated driver came from behind, weaving in and out of his lane as he fixated on the scene; and rather than avoiding the parked car, he slammed into its rear— pinning Stella precariously between the two.

She lay bleeding on the pavement in a state of shock, but her mind was strangely clear. Stella could sense she was dying. Lying in a puddle of water reddened with her own blood, she heard a voice so distinctive she could only describe it as "harsh but gentle, at once tough and yet also kind." In that deep clarity where life hangs in the balance, she knew it was the Lord. She was so certain, in fact, that she spoke what she felt was obvious, "Oh, I guess you are here to take me home."

Then, without thinking, she added, "But I'm not finished with the baby books yet." (Evidently, Stella was a serious scrapbooker.)

Stella reports that she heard a "mighty, strong, and joyous laugh." The next words were reassuring and clear. "Stella, you aren't going to die . . . but your life is going to be very different."

Stella survived this traumatic evening though she lost both of her legs in the accident. I first encountered her story in the local paper. I read and reread the account, noting that even a skeptical news reporter could not resist reporting word for word the conversation of this credible woman as God met her in a moment of *in extremis*.

My husband and I now attend Stella's church. I see her regularly. She makes her way around on carefully crafted stilts, and sometimes you forget they aren't her legs. Her face is a picture of courage and joy.

I cannot help but marvel at Stella's unique encounter with the Lord and the gracious way he prepared her for such a radical change. She reminds me that bad things do happen to good people, but even the worst things look different when we are *aware* of God's presence.

## IF WE HAD EARS TO HEAR

I know it sounds so Sunday schoolish—like the first idea you communicate to a roomful of squirming five-year-olds. *God is with you.* These words must be terribly important though. Nearly every angel in Scripture who comes to deliver a message to anyone—from reluctant warriors like Gideon to bewildered shepherds on the hill-sides of Bethlehem—says in the same, broken-record fashion, *Do not fear, for the Lord is with you.* It's as though God is trying to get through to us and we have cotton in our ears.

*We will never believe he is enough until we know he understands.*

The God of Abraham and Isaac and Jacob, who will one day gather all of history under his glorious banner—the God who created every intricate neuron in our brains, has stepped into our experience and declared that we are not alone. Do not fear . . . for the Lord is with you.

Now I admit that it would be easier to walk through life

with the awareness of God's presence if we had an experience like Stella's. But that is precisely my point—God is every bit as present in our lives. We are only less aware.

I question, sometimes, if we can ever grasp the wonder that God is with us—with us through thick and thin—until we face the immovable. Perhaps it is only a churchy phrase before that point. But a state of unrelenting singleness with no man on the horizon . . . or a child who makes the same poor decision over and over may not be a bad dream from which you necessarily awake. It could well be reality. Here the great question of our lives turns a corner. Is God really enough for this, whatever this is? I mean . . . *is he really enough?* We will never believe he is enough until we know he understands.

Most of us have someone in our lives—a husband or sister, a good friend or our mother—that we'd trade half our savings to feel as though that person really understood us. Perhaps you know what this picture is like. You describe in telling detail (or maybe you just hint in colorful subtlety) some situation where there's a lot at stake. You feel a bit desperate. This is important. Or something has happened that threatens what you hold dear. And if the other person has any clue, he tries to understand—to climb behind your eyes and see it, or find a corner of his heart and feel it the way you do.

But you can tell because you, too, have a clue: he doesn't get it. What you are feeling is outside his frame of reference. You are speaking in French—but he can only hear Spanish. Or the worst of all possibilities can be the plain truth of the matter. He doesn't really care. You might be dying on the inside, but his mind is somewhere else. If you know what it is to long for someone you love to understand you deeply, then the empathy and understanding of God holds special importance for you.

Isaiah, who foresaw the suffering of Christ, seemed to grasp this. He writes in the clearest, most direct words, lest we miss his point:

*In all their affliction He was afflicted.* (Isa. 63:9)

The God of Israel, he explains, actually feels the affliction of your afflictions, the difficulty of your difficulties, because he has been where you are. He is not some version of a Greek god, the Zeus of your childhood stories, who stands removed, passionless, and uncaring.

The Psalms echo this theme many times in words that are probably familiar to your ears. "The LORD is gracious and full

*God feels with you in a way no human being can begin to touch. He gets it.*

of compassion" (Ps. 111:4, 112:4, and 145:8 KJV). The Hebrew word for *compassion,* though, is not some sweet, feel-good pat on the back. It means to be kicked in the gut. God feels with you in a way no human being can begin to touch. He gets it. He entered your frame of reference, took on the limitations of your flesh, the weariness that settles in your spirit. "We need not wonder how God feels because in Jesus,

God gave us a face."[2] We have only to feel our way through the life of Christ to believe that he knows. Dear God, how he knows.

Can you picture the places in your own heart where you become undone—and no one knows, really, except you and God? Something that another woman might soar on past unearths your particular vulnerability—it pushes your buttons. It might be a series of small defeats and frustrations that you should overcome easily, you feel, but you haven't.

*What would it be like to go through this experience with God?*

What would change in your heart if you could believe that God is there on that very path, waiting for you, and that he understands the struggle in all its intimate detail?

The truth is that it's rarely what happens to us that determines our future. It's the conclusions we draw in secret that pin us to the wall. *Somehow, I've just got to manage this muck as best I can.* As John Stott writes:

> . . . the real sting of suffering is not the misfortune itself, nor even the pain or injustice of it, but the apparent God-forsakenness of it. Pain is endurable, but the seeming indifference of God is not.[3]

If we see ourselves as struggling through alone, we are in the most vulnerable state of all.

## A CRUCIAL DIFFERENCE

When real nail-biting difficulties come our way, most of us enter a kind of spiritual twilight zone where the profound truths of our faith are still true—they are just not true about us. Not now, and not in the middle of this. *I can believe that God is with me, that his power and his mercy will carry me through this—when I can get to a better place.* Until then . . . well, we've just got to manage.

I remember thinking when Emily told me her story that she could be speaking the thoughts of any woman on a bad day—of me, on a bad day. Many of us secretly fear what she feared. All of a sudden, it seemed, things in Emily's life had broken loose. Her mother was dying and her middle schooler was struggling in ways she couldn't fix and her husband's crushing schedule kept him gone. She was discouraged and starting to wake up in the middle of the night. Yet that was not her big concern.

"I'm scared," Emily confessed. I thought she was afraid of what was happening with her daughter—or what life might be like without her mother. But her fear had a different source.

"I'm afraid I'm failing *the test*," she went on to explain. "I have all these years in Bible studies and prayer groups. Others look to me for answers—and I can give them pretty good ones. I shouldn't be struggling like this."

In Emily's mind, her struggle meant that she was a spiritual failure. "I'm just not on top of my game," was how she put it. Somehow this was the great test of her life . . . and she was failing. I ventured a question that is the same question I ask myself in moments like this—when my expectations for myself or others actually exceed God's: What would it be like to go through this experience *with God*?

The situation may not change—or at least, not anytime soon. But if God is really with me, then I move from a courtroom where judgment is pronounced or a track meet with winners and losers—to a journey. This is not a test. And God doesn't have a grading pen. The picture is much closer to the one these song lyrics express:

> Imagine a King who would come through the darkness
> And walk where I walk, full of greatness,
> And call me to His side,
> Just like a Father and child.[4]

If the King has come and he walks with us, then the uncertainty or grief or fear becomes the actual subject of conversation. We are in the company of the risen Christ . . . who is better than any father we have ever known. That's why those who experienced his companionship over many years could sing, "What a *friend* we have in Jesus, all our sins and griefs to bear."[5] The empathy of Jesus—of being with God—was just that real.

## IN THE WORST MOMENTS

If someone asked you about the hardest times or worst moments in your life, I suspect you'd find the emotional content largely centered on one of three things: feeling betrayed, experiencing a deep sense of loss, or being humiliated in some way.[6] That's where the pain of life is felt in its sharpest, most stinging ways.

It's really important to be able to name the worst moments in your story—not to set up camp there but to let those moments become an emotional window into the experience of Christ. You must find the worst moments in your story . . . in his story. Something mysterious in your own experience gets quietly transformed there. And you will discover that you doubt far less that God knows what's happening in your life . . . or that he cares.

## BETRAYAL

Betrayal is what we all feel when we discover a good friend didn't include us in the dinner party or said something that put us in a bad light. It's surely what a woman feels when the man with whom she's shared bed and board is willing to throw away twenty years of marriage and family. It begs the response, "But I thought you would be here for me" or "I thought we were friends."

Who among us hasn't felt, at some point, betrayed by someone we love? And if we're honest, who hasn't left someone else twisting in the wind of that experience? Betrayal is really a matter of looking out for my own interests first—even if someone else gets hurt.

The theme of betrayal is everywhere in the story of Jesus. Do you see his pain as he rides into Jerusalem on a donkey, knowing that the cries of those who shout "Hosanna!" on this day will be the same voices who shout "Crucify him!" the next? Can you feel the stab Jesus feels when he was completely alone, and his close friend Peter looks him in the eye and says, "I never knew this man"?

Have you let it take your breath away? If you do—if you ask God to help you understand what Jesus experienced— you will never feel quite as alone in your own story again. The betrayal you've known is your ticket to that understanding. And the sweetness of knowing that he knows is what slowly pulls the splinter out of your own heart.

## LOSS

In many ways, life is one loss after the other—from cradle to grave. From the moment we first scoot off our mother's lap, we are letting go and being let go of. The losses that linger— the big ones that shape our lives—are those in which what's lost is irreplaceable.

I remember talking with the mother of two sons, one living and one dead. "How did your son die?" I asked her.

She paused for a moment before she answered. "About five years ago, my sons were on a hunting trip—and the older accidentally shot the younger," she explained.

My mouth fell open. It's hard enough to lose one son. But to know how deep the emotional scars would run for the son who survived is doubly tragic. "How have you made it?" I asked her when I could find words.

She admitted there were times when she wondered if she

would make it through this. "The turning point," she said, "was when I realized that God lost a Son too. He was no stranger to this. And even more, I saw that the loss that I was feeling was pain that God chose. *He chose this pain.* That still amazes me. I slowly began to believe that God would bear this loss in me."

If you look at the life of Christ through the lens of loss, you see that from the moment of incarnation to his last breath, he took on every human grief. Someone once pictured it as Christ littering heaven with his glory, so much was he leaving behind. In a peasant girl's dark womb, in those agonizing moments when he felt his Father's absence, there is no place in human experience—in our experience—that Jesus has not been.

> *There is no place in human experience—in our experience—that Jesus has not been.*

## HUMILIATION

To feel the sting of something that humiliates you is to be dipped into the experience of shame—the most toxic of all emotions. It could be the loss of a job or the loss of a love, or something as small as a few critical words, and feelings of shame are triggered. Somehow you feel exposed. Weighed in the balance and found wanting. *Humiliated.* It's such a miserable experience that generally, we avoid it at all costs.

Women whose backgrounds include sexual abuse have taught me much about the shaping influence of shame, because shame is the core experience of sexual abuse. A friend I'll call Stephanie explained to me once how she felt for the longest time she was carrying inside her "a white-hot ball of anger" toward the men in her life. Her brother, and later her step-

*When we find our deepest struggles embedded in the suffering face of Jesus, our hearts slowly melt and our lives change in ways we could never force into being.*

father, had slipped into her bedroom growing up. "It took the longest time for me to see that my anger was really the face of shame. I just felt so humiliated by their advances —like I was this worthless little girl a man saw for only one purpose."

Stephanie came to a point in her journey with God where she had to get the rawness of these emotions out in the open. She found herself praying the question she knew had been there all along. "Where were you, God, when all this happened to me?"

She could feel all the anger and shame push its way to the top, like an infection that needed to be lanced. Not usually one to just pick up the Bible and read randomly, on this occasion Stephanie did that. The page that fell open on her lap was, of all things, a passage from Psalm 22, which records the private experience of Jesus on the cross.

> Be not far from me, for trouble is near;
> For there is none to help.

Many bulls have surrounded me;
Strong bulls of Bashan have encircled me.
They open wide their mouth at me.
As a ravening and a roaring lion. (vv. 11–13)

Stephanie explains that for the first time, the nakedness and powerlessness that Jesus experienced in his suffering became real to her. Where was God when all this was happening in her life? He was agonizing on a cross—bearing in his body the weight of her own grief and humiliation.

I struggle for words to explain why this makes a difference. After all, the sexual abuse still happened. The mother of two boys in a hunting accident still has only one son left living. There are things in your life—and in mine—that we both wish would never have taken place. And yet what I do know is that when we find our deepest struggles embedded in the suffering face of Jesus, our hearts slowly melt and our lives change in ways we could never force into being.

Martha's pointed question of Jesus—as she labored in the kitchen while Mary sat at his feet—is one we feel less need to ask: "Lord, don't you care?" (Luke 10:40 NIV). After all, the home of Martha was Christ's last stop on his way to Jerusalem. Dinner around her table was his last warm evening with friends before he faced the Cross.

If we find our worst moments in the worst moments of Christ, we ask less often if he cares because we know. We know.

## IN THE ORDINARY MOMENTS

So, yes, there are huge moments in our lives when, like Stella, we are pinned between immovable realities and the question is, can we let ourselves become aware that God is with us?

I should add here that once again, if entitlement stalks our soul and deep down we feel we should be exempt from hard things and suffering places, then experiencing the empathy of God will remain forever elusive. If somehow I think that being a Christian should get me a bigger slice of the good life, if Jesus suffered so I don't have to—then I am in danger of missing the very best part, which is *his fellowship in the journey.* His presence in the lonely places. His joy where there's little humanly to be had.

> *If somehow I think that being a Christian should get me a bigger slice of the good life, if Jesus suffered so I don't have to—then I am in danger of missing the very best part, which is* his fellowship in the journey.

Letting ourselves become aware that God is with us, that he is truly present—this is the issue at stake. He *is* truly present . . . but will we allow ourselves to take that in?

I suspect that, like many women, my greater struggle is recognizing the common moments, the dinky details that would remind me (if I let them) that I'm not alone on this path—that God is truly with me. Not out there when my dreams come true. Not when my devotional life is finally what it ought to be. But now . . . here . . . in this place and in this moment, God is with me.

A few years back, I stumbled on a simple experience that got my attention in this regard. My husband was driving me to the airport to catch a plane to speak at a women's weekend. Only it was snowing, and I was late getting my act together. I am the kind of woman who finds it easier to speak at the conference than to get there with her toothbrush. It's the rounding up of all the accoutrements that makes me crazy.

So here is my midwestern husband edging his way carefully on icy roads, trying to dodge all the native Southerners who can't drive in the snow. And it hits me—I left my pajamas. Once again, I left my pajamas at home.

"Honey," I venture, "do you think we could turn around and go back? We're five minutes from home, and I forgot my pajamas."

"Pau-la," he replies, enunciating carefully lest I fail to catch his drift, "we are not turning around. It is snow-ing."

I sigh. Another weekend freezing between a set of sheets. Oh well, there are worse things. I make peace with my annoying inability to manage details.

Often the women who organize a weekend such as this leave a little basket of goodies in your room. Sometimes there are a few flowers to welcome you. Chocolate is not unusual. Note cards or candles or bottles of water—these are the usual items you might find by your bedside.

On this occasion—and none other since then—I found a gift I unwrapped only to discover, to my complete surprise, a pair of pajamas. My size, my style, picked out two weeks prior on a sudden whim by a woman who thought, *Let's do something different this year!*

I keep these pajamas in my suitcase now. They are my traveling set—I freeze between strange sheets no more. But far more important, these pajamas remind me to pay attention. God was nudging me awake, trying to get me to recognize his obvious presence in the small details of life—which, in my rush for the extraordinary, I tend to barrel right on past.

I wonder, sometimes, how many sets of pajamas do we miss in our lives? In the consoling words of a friend, or a verse from Scripture that seems to be highlighted, or a song on the radio that touches some deep place of longing in you . . . do you hear his voice? Do you sense his presence with you? The novelist John Updike once said that he had not received some beatific vision of God,

> *These ordinary moments are God's whispers. Can you hear them?*

but rather, he'd heard "whispers from the wings of the stage."[7] These ordinary moments are God's whispers. Can you hear them? In a real way, we could say that prayer and Scripture are, perhaps, the more obvious means of staying aware of God's presence. They help us pay attention.

That's especially true if we are bringing our actual lives— what's really happening in us—to those pages. Listen to the way Eugene Peterson translates a familiar passage from the Gospel of Matthew:

"Here's what I want you to do: Find a quiet, secluded place so you won't be tempted to role-play before God. Just be there as simply and honestly as you can manage. The focus will shift from you to God, and you will begin to sense his grace." (Matt. 6:6 MSG)

*Just be there as simply and honestly as you can manage . . . and you will begin to sense his grace.* His presence with you is his grace. You will know where to go and what to do from here—from this moment where you let yourself become aware of his compassion, his empathy, his glory as it lives in you in Christ. He is with you. It is that simple—and that amazing.

I have always loved the refrain woven through Psalm 46, like a drumbeat we march to or a Hebrew chant to be sung. It says simply, "The LORD of hosts is with us; The God of Jacob is our stronghold" (vv. 7, 11).

*He is with you. It is that simple—and that amazing.*

A friend once pointed out that there are two names for God in these verses, which, if we understood them, would tell us much about Who is actually with us. The Lord of hosts is Christ, the captain of all the angelic armies of heaven. God, in all his mighty power, is with us.

But the second name for God holds even greater mystery. *The God of Jacob* is the name by which God refers to himself more often than any other name used in the Bible. That is worth a long pause. Of those three patriarchs—Abraham and

Isaac and Jacob—would you choose to align yourself with Jacob? The broken man who schemed and manipulated his way into his inheritance—the man who walked with a limp because he wrestled with God? Yet God calls himself the God of Jacob. He identifies himself as the God of broken people— like you and me.[8]

There in those two verses is our crowning glory. The very power of heaven, Christ in his victory and triumph, walks with us. All the compassion and mercy of the God of Jacob, the God of broken people—it is he who is at our side.

# WAITING WITH JESUS

*"My soul is deeply grieved, to the point of death;*
*remain here and keep watch with Me."*
—MATTHEW 26:38

The actual experience of Christ as he journeyed toward the Cross often gets lost in a theological understanding that keeps us removed—and therefore unable to connect our own experience with Christ.

In this exercise, turn to a scene that may be familiar to you. It's the night before Christ faces the Cross. He has been to dinner with his friends, sitting at the same table with the man who would betray him. One of his best friends, Peter, insists that he will never turn his back on Jesus—and Jesus tells him a cock will crow after the third time he does exactly that.

Now Christ comes, late at night, to a garden where he often goes to pray. It is his wish that his friends would stay awake with him. As you read the account in Matthew 26:36–46, let yourself be there on that hillside and see what you discover as you wait with Jesus.

What part of Christ's struggle here do you feel the most? In what ways does he seem profoundly alone in these moments?

Take a few moments to write—and then to pray—about moments in your life when you've felt one small part of what Christ is feeling in this scene.

What changes in your own experience as you find yourself identified with Jesus—and him with you?

*Chapter 8*

# LOVING (DIFFICULT) PEOPLE

## FINDING THE FREEDOM TO LOVE

> *It is much easier to preach the gospel of love for mankind*
> *than it is to love single, individual,*
> *and not very lovable sinners.*
> —WILLIAM BARCLAY

> *But now, thus says the LORD, your Creator, O Jacob,*
> *And He who formed you, O Israel,*
> *"Do not fear, for I have redeemed you;*
> *I have called you by name; you are Mine!"*
> —ISAIAH 43:1

*Marie would say that she feels trapped in a marriage with a* wounded man—a nice-enough guy who grew up on various army posts where his father was stationed.

Her husband's idea of loving her is, understandably, a variation on that very theme. He gives directions—lots of them. There is a certain way to vacuum and particular vitamins he wants her to take. Her thoughts on politics she learned to keep to herself a few years back. Her husband would tell you that the world is a harsh place, and he is being protective.

133

Marie, however, feels smothered. Perhaps you would encourage her to gently insist that surely her husband has more important things to focus on besides carpet and vitamins—there are bigger fish to fry in life. You'd tell Marie she needs more breathing room, and she would quickly agree.

It's just that saying something like that to her husband makes him angry. Not the explosive stuff anyone would call a halt to—but the sullen, frozen retreat of a man who can't name his anger and would not have a clue to its origin. He just kind of goes away.

For Marie, it's so self-defeating. What she wants, like a little girl starved for a good meal, is a bit of tenderness from this man whose heart she felt she knew when they first met. Mind you—she's not asking for the moon. *Honey, that was an incredible meal.* She could live on a remark like that for days. *You've got a great brain . . . why not take a class on something that interests you?* If only he could see her—actually notice who she is—perhaps she could see herself. She waits for words like that. She is still waiting.

Marie would admit that she fantasizes about leaving her husband. She wants an escape from feeling trapped. But her faith suggests there must be other options. Her husband does love her, in his own way. And the children—she will not do that to her children.

Recently, Marie has found herself praying a bit differently. She is asking God for freedom of a different sort. *Lord, is there some way you can free me from within?* she wonders.

## LONGING FOR SOMETHING
## THAT NEVER QUITE COMES

I know lots of Maries. Almost without exception, we've all had a *difficult* person in our lives and sometimes more than one. (Of course, each of us can be difficult on a bad day.)

But this is about something deeper than a bad day. The truth is that we enter our adult lives with a dream we're not aware of. The dream is this: somewhere along our path, a living person will step forward and bestow on us a sort of blessing—a deep validation that sticks to our ribs and washes away all previous crud. We cannot name this, but we look for it. Oh, how we look for it.

The illusion is that if we just had the deep approval of our best friend or our mother or some man who really matters— we would soar. We'd have the confidence to tackle nearly anything. The holes in our soul would fill in with good stuff. It would be the healing of an old, old ache.

Here the plotline thickens. For inevitably, it seems, the person who matters most is oddly unable—or unwilling— to bestow the blessing we

> *The illusion is that if we just had the deep approval of our best friend or our mother or some man who really matters—we would soar.*

need. And when this happens, that person becomes a *difficult person*. A rather macabre dance ensues. You try harder to get the person's approval—and it only proves more elusive. I sometimes think of it as relational proof that, indeed, the universe is fallen.

Lots of us who could name a difficult person in our lives are Roman gladiators at heart—meaning, we look to the thumbs-up or thumbs-down of some invisible audience who can determine our fate . . . and our worth. When that picture describes our relational world, escape will look very good. We will let that difficult friendship go. We'll see our mother far less often. Our hearts will shrink into such a search for self-preservation that we won't be able to love well. And worst of all, we will miss what God has longed to give us all along.

## WHAT MAKES A PERSON DIFFICULT?

Perhaps I should share that Marie also had a good friend. They met in a babysitting co-op when their children were toddlers. Marie shared a lot of her dreams and hopes with this particular friend, especially a desire to go to graduate school. She regretted her earlier decision to be a nurse. But school seemed like a huge mountain to cross at this point in life. Marie longed for her friend's encouragement. *You can do it!* If she had someone to cheer her on, she could build up her courage and take a few classes.

Only her friend had her own passel of insecurities, and academics was right at top of the list. "It might be hard to juggle school and home," was the best she could produce.

All of this is to say—we meet difficult people in various

shapes along life's path. But our struggle is not really with these people.

The reason a relationship feels difficult is that the person has become the living embodiment of the voices in your head. She taps into insecurities already roosting within. Her lack of approval or validation triggers a chorus line of inner complaint—it disturbs the little girl in you who uses any excuse to remind you what she deeply believes:

*If you were just smarter, thinner, prettier, holier, or at least a better mother . . . you'd feel like Somebody. You'd meet with more applause. Your parking ticket would be stamped, and then you could make your way onto the freeway of life with all the other grown-ups.*

That may sound a bit strong. But honestly, when you peel back the layers of a person you find difficult to love—of a relationship that feels intolerable—this is the white noise in the background of your soul. It's true for all of us. We can be paralyzed by the power we give someone to name us.

For a long time, the human tendency is to try harder—to perform or reform or otherwise turn life into a juggling act. And usually, as the dance goes, for a thousand reasons, they cannot deliver the validation you would want.

That can be a great disappointment. Like Marie felt, it's tempting to exit the relationship entirely. When the blessing or the approval or the encouragement just isn't there in sufficient quantities, it can be a real disappointment.

Or it can spring your trap and spell your freedom.

## THE GYMNASIUM OF YOUR SOUL

Enter God. For like it or not, God is tugging at our hearts in this difficult place. He is calling out to us through a stuck relationship, where we can't love well because we are waiting to be loved. Waiting and waiting.

Look at the carrot he dangles in front of us, the promise hidden in the fine print—which, honestly, is one of the richest aspects of losing some of your dreams and expectations . . . and finding yourself on this journey with him. The apostle Paul writes that Jesus is the One who gives us a place to stand in his grace, where we anticipate the glory of God. And then, like a man who suddenly breaks into song, he adds:

> And not only this, but we also exult in our tribulations, knowing that tribulation brings about perseverance; and perseverance, proven character; and proven character, hope; *and hope does not disappoint, because the love of God has been poured out within our hearts* . . . (Rom. 5:3–5; emphasis added)

Behind the door of your frustration, there is a huge hope— a hope so free and exuberant it could only be pictured as a colt or a calf finally released from a cramped stall where it has been pinned (Mal. 4:2).

The hope is that quite possibly, there is a greater love than you could guess, so lavish you could drown in it—a love God does not hold back on, a love he willingly pours in and through you. This hope does not disappoint (it's actually the only hope that doesn't) because no matter what happens to you—no matter what difficult people come into your life—it can only take you a bit deeper into the inexhaustible love of God. There's always more where that came from, so to speak.

So what does this say about the impossible person in your life? It means that God has placed this person in your path for a reason. God wants to spring the lock on the cage of disapproval or rejection you've lived in—not necessarily by removing this particular human voice, but rather by allowing you to hear his more clearly.

I sometimes think of a difficult relationship as a gymnasium for the soul. Learning to stand your ground when you need to—or forgive when it's a challenge to forgive—being able to see the broken person inside a tough exterior is like lifting a twenty-pound weight. It can be hard work. It totally presses you into the heart of the Father. But every time you work out in this gym, so to speak, you grow

*He is calling out to us through a stuck relationship, where we can't love well because we are waiting to be loved.*

a stronger layer of fiber within. You become a little more solid inside. The real woman you are—the woman God has made and Jesus died for—she lives! This woman, who is already loved by Christ, is able to love someone without much flowing back to her.

*Fearless vulnerability.* That's the best name I know for this soul fiber, and truly, it spells freedom. It is a sweaty struggle to learn to love when loving is not easy. But if you consider the strength and courage and empathy these trips to the gym build in your life, you'd be inclined to send a thank-you note.

## A PLACE OF ABUNDANCE

There's a passage hidden in the Psalms that describes what this gymnasium feels like—and where it leads. Notice the weighty imagery and the intended result of this process.

> Bless our God, O peoples,
> And sound His praise abroad,
> Who keeps us in life
> And does not allow our feet to slip.
> For You have tried us, O God;
> You have refined us as silver is refined.
> You brought us into the net;
> You laid an oppressive burden upon our loins.
> You made men ride over our heads;
> We went through fire and through water,
> *Yet You brought us out into a place of abundance.*
> (Ps. 66:8–12; emphasis added)

The abundance God is drawing you toward is almost like a physical place—it's a space on the inside where *you have detached yourself* from everyone in your past and anyone in your present whose opinion holds too much power. It's like serving notice. You are grabbing hold of what is real and true: *only God can name me.* And he absolutely reserves that right.

There is a real you in there whom only God knows—an actual *you* he created and loved from before the world began. To be this woman, a woman whom Jesus loves, is enough. It will carry you all the way home, if you let it.

Sometimes, when I am in the gym of my own soul and longing to rest in this place where I am already loved (and thus not needing a human stamp of approval), I am drawn back to C. S. Lewis's beloved children's story *The Lion, the Witch and the Wardrobe.* This may be the most famous children's story of the last hundred years, and for good reason.

Perhaps you remember what it's like when the White Witch comes on the scene—it's always winter but never Christmas. Her evil spell is called *deep magic from the dawn of time.* I can hardly think of a better phrase to describe the belief that without some particular person's love and approval, I am lost and undone. When those old voices appear to win, it's an awful spell. We are in a trance, waiting and hoping for a human mirror in which to look and see ourselves whole and loved. Indeed, it seems like a winter where there's no Christmas.

But do you also remember how you feel in the story when Aslan finally appears and the ice begins to thaw? What a moment! It fascinates me that Lewis titled Aslan's chapter with such telling words: "Deeper Magic from Before the Dawn of Time." Lewis is pulling us past every person and event on the surface of our experience. He wants us to listen through the noise: there is a Voice, and that Voice predates every negative voice in your head. His deeper magic is truth. No abuse can undo it. No condemning words in your past absolutely have to shape your future. There is a deeper magic, and it's unspeakably strong stuff.

We have been ushered into life with an invitation engraved in blood, delivered in the body of a suffering God with our names on his lips.

> *You are grabbing hold of what is real and true: only God can name me.*

The road home, always, is allowing myself to be brought back to this simple place over and over again—and often by the impetus of a difficult relationship. I let the love and blessing of Christ on my life be enough because it is. I get captivated by the deepest magic of all. I hear him name me as his own—and I let that stick to my ribs.

When I do, it no longer feels like someone is standing on my air hose. My life and my worth are not at the mercy of any human being. From here, I can actually offer myself to others with a measure of unconscious abandon. I get to give a teaspoon of the very love that's flowing through me.

That, I realize, is the magic at its very best.

## THE FACE OF LOVE

It's fair to ask how our Father's love plays out in our relationships. If difficult people and trying situations become places where we taste the love of God, then how does this translate into a love felt by others? That is the point, actually. The goal of everything we learn about God is "love from a pure heart and a good conscience and a sincere faith" (1 Tim. 1:5). *Yes, love from a pure heart.* But what does that mean?

I would suggest that as our dreams in life are transformed, one of the best gifts is a growing ability to love others. We can understand when we are not understood. We can give when there's not a lot coming our way. There is something flowing through us we did not manufacture. It could be best described by a few abilities that seem to grow over time.

## THE GRACE TO HOLD PEOPLE LIGHTLY

The phrase *hold people lightly* is an old one, born of the truth that God brings certain individuals into your life for a season. No one stays permanently. Friends move away or find other friends. Children grow up and leave home. Even a spouse eventually dies. In the familiar words of Ecclesiastes, "To everything there is a season, a time for every purpose under heaven" (3:1 NKJV).

But if my life is rooted in the love of Christ, then friendships and relationships are what they are—gifts for a season to be received and enjoyed. If I cling or hold on for dear life, the relationship will crumble in my hand. If I hold people lightly, my friend is not required to take my advice or accept my help. I can love someone without pulling from her more than she wants to give. Holding people lightly is a huge part of loving well.

## THE COURAGE TO LOVE SOMEONE BOLDLY

If you think back to Marie's story, you know that her fan-
tasies about leaving her husband were really a call to courage.

Anyone in a friendship or a relationship that's stuck—
*really* stuck—knows what fortitude it takes to say, "We've got
to do this dance a little differently. We're both dying here." Yet
how do we know that this kind of courage is truly the face of
love? Why isn't it love to simply continue to accommodate, to
tiptoe on eggshells, to keep dancing in place?

Marie's story is a great example. Her husband's smother-
ing protectiveness was really the mirror of his own fear.
Somehow, he thought he'd lose what he loved if he did not
hold it with a death grip of control. And Christ was there,
seeking to pry his fingers loose. If Marie had just kept dancing the same old dance, her husband would have never discovered God as the Father he can count on. To love her
husband well, Marie had to say things like, "Honey, we've
got to talk about what makes it so hard for you to offer a
word of encouragement. We've got to talk about choices I
need to be making for myself. Something in this picture
brings back all your fear."

Our misery is meant to lead us to the courage we need.
We have to find Christ as the Source of our identity and worth.
That will often stretch someone we love where they need to
be stretched. It's a regular blue-light, two-for-one special—
and that's why it's love. It provides the other person's ticket
home, too, if he wants to take it.

Indeed, courage is the face of love when it invites the other person into growth and freedom—which, for a Christian, means that you are learning to actively trust God in places where old fears and insecurities have controlled you.

## THE HUMILITY OF ACCEPTING PEOPLE WHERE THEY ARE

Have you ever wondered how Christ could look at a person and know all that was in her heart—and still love her? Being free to love others well inches us along that same path, for no one in our lives is totally a white knight or a wicked witch. We're a mixture of the good, the bad, and the ugly. Or in the words of Eudora Welty, a novelist known for piercing insight into human nature, "People are mostly layers of violence and tenderness wrapped like bulbs, and it is difficult to say what makes them onions or hyacinths."[1]

Isn't that an incredible way to describe people? All of us are layers of violence and tenderness—and sometimes, we smell more like an onion than a flower.

For this reason the Bible says, very simply, that part of love is taking people where they are. "Accept one another, just as Christ also accepted us to the glory of God," Paul wrote (Rom. 15:7).

Sometimes acceptance leads to the greatest miracle of all—just being able to hang in there with someone. God enlarges your heart to hold the good and the bad in one container. You can respect someone's strength and yet also see his insecurities as part of the same package. Bearing with someone allows you to see his stony silence as a reflection of the broken, scared kid in him. Less and less can you be fooled into thinking his response is always and inevitably a reflection of you.

It's easier to love someone who's an onion one week and a hyacinth the next if you understand that, usually, it's not about you.

## LEARNING TO LOVE AS A GROWN-UP

Let me fill in a few missing pieces from Marie's life. Her story shows some of the rich places that learning to love freely can take us—and why it's often better than our original dream.

Marie did make it through graduate school. Her husband is still overprotective, though he slowly recognized his real fear: that his wife would find herself and no longer need him. As he learned to trust God with his future, he actually became one of her biggest cheerleaders.

> *The deepest magic of the Cross is what shapes this woman you are.*

Something else happened, though, as Marie got older—something she never imagined. Other women turned to her for encouragement. At first, she had to fight the urge to run. *What do they see in me?* she wondered. She had flashbacks of her own mother—a depressed, reclusive woman who chain-smoked through the anxiety of a life that felt overwhelming. Marie saw herself as having little to offer other women. She felt she needed mothering herself.

So Marie began to do something that felt a little strange at first. She offered what she could to the women God brought into her life—a listening ear, a word of empathy, a simple meal in a hard time. More importantly, she let God mother her. From being loved, she learned how to love.

"It seems like a small miracle to be able to give what I didn't get," she once said to me.

What's better than the dreams we try to cart through life? It has something to do with this—the way God enlarges the spaces in our own cramped hearts so others actually find a refuge there. The freedom to move out into life because God has called you there, and that's enough. The discovery that you have something to offer others out of the truth born in you. The deepest magic of the Cross is what shapes this woman you are.

Sometimes I picture Jesus there, in his suffering, looking out onto a sea of human faces, ours among them. What did he see? Some were in agony at his pain. Others gloated over his defeat. Some gawked in open disgust. But what did Jesus see in those faces? I think he saw people he loved. And he never stopped loving them—not for a moment. His heart is so beyond my own; I cannot comprehend such compassion. So I find myself asking, simply, "Lord, would you give me some shred of your heart for people in my life? Could I have a tiny drop from your infinite supply of love?"

He is more than willing—always willing. In the long run, I suspect we'll discover that the people we call *difficult* are the ones God most uses to purchase our freedom from prisons we hardly knew we inhabited. I think we'll look back and say that learning to love out of a heart set free is, indeed, the only hope that does not fail.

# HAVING AN "I'VE-COME-TO-REALIZE" CONVERSATION

*Thus says the LORD, your Redeemer, the Holy One of Israel,*
*"I am the LORD your God who teaches you to profit,*
*Who leads you in the way you should go."*
—ISAIAH 48:17

In a difficult relationship, the tendency is to wait for the other person to make changes—to simply supply the approval or affirmation you long for. Yet God often works in a different way. More specifically, he uses the truth you speak in the presence of this person to release something deep in you. In owning that truth with another, you actually start to believe the truth about you for yourself. This is called an *I've-come-to-realize* conversation.

There are two parts to this conversation. First, you will want to write a short paragraph about what you always believed about yourself in the midst of a difficult relationship.

*I never saw myself as enough of this or that . . .*
*I could not believe that I was able to . . .*
*In this person's presence, I always felt . . .*

Then write a second short paragraph about the truth God has shown you.

*I've come to realize that (this particular truth or reality)*
*is closer to the truth of who I am in Christ . . .*

Now (and this is the hard but freeing part), simply pray for and take the first good opportunity God gives with this particular person to say that there are a few things you have begun to realize about your own life . . . and then describe those briefly.

Notice that in this conversation, you are not making any accusations—you are not asking for feedback or even a different response. You are simply stating something important you've come to realize about yourself and how you've approached relationships. What matters is that your own ears hear the truth . . . in the presence of someone with whom you've lived a different story.

# THE PLEASURE OF
# HIS COMPANY

# Chapter 9

# THE PLACE MEANT FOR YOU

## DISCOVERING THE JOY OF
## YOUR SMALL PART

> *To grow up*
> *is to find*
> *the small part you are playing*
> *in this extraordinary drama*
> *written by*
> *somebody else.*
> —MADELEINE L'ENGLE

> *Thanks be to God, who always leads us*
> *in triumph in Christ, and manifests through us*
> *the sweet aroma of the knowledge of Him in every place.*
> —2 CORINTHIANS 2:14

*Perhaps you know how awkward it feels, sometimes, when* you meet someone for the first time and about ten minutes into the conversation, the question appears: "So what do you do?" Depending on the season of your life, you fish around for some way to explain what you currently *do*. Surely there is some label that makes sense—some tag that describes the way you spend your days.

At many points in my life, I've found that a hard question. A woman's life has always seemed more complicated than a couple of neat labels can explain adequately. But I've noticed that as I've traveled farther in this journey with God, my own focus has changed shape. It matters less what I do out there in the world. The real question becomes more like *what am I meant to give?*

You can sense that there is a place you are meant to occupy—there are lives that wait to be touched with the love of Christ as it is poured through you. The real question is, how do we recognize this niche with our name on it?

In *Strong Women, Soft Hearts* I told the story of a woman who, out of the pain of her own past, volunteered half a day a week in a pregnancy life center counseling women who were considering whether to give birth to a child—or have an abortion.[1] When I questioned how she, a single mother of two small children, could spare that kind of time, she looked at me strangely and spoke words that have shaped my own understanding of calling and contribution. "Oh, Paula," she said, "when I work with women who are weighing out the choice to give life, I feel like I'm doing something I was born for."

As much as she regretted her past choices, she knew that her place in the great scheme of things was helping other women weigh out the gravity of giving a child life. An afternoon with women facing unwanted pregnancies was a highlight in her week.

Her phrase has resonated with me for many years: "I'm doing something I was born for."

Am I listening to God's tug on my heart and letting my feet follow? *Am I doing what I was born for?* How does a woman ever know?

Frederick Buechner says that there is a hidden intersection in life—the converging of two separate forces—and the spot where they meet has your name on it. He explains it this way: "The place God has for you is the place where your deep gladness and the world's deep hunger meet."[2]

I love the simplicity of that statement. I think it's the true bull's-eye of where we're meant to be in life. Find what makes your heart sing and how that

> *The real question becomes more like what am I meant to give?*

touches the sea of need around you—that niche will feel like something that's been prepared for you. It won't necessarily be easy. But there's joy there, a sense of deep satisfaction.

## LIVING WHAT YOU'RE BORN FOR

I want to introduce you to a woman whose story mirrors this reality. Jesse Copeland is an elderly black woman, southern to the bone, and though she's a legend in these parts, she will never grace the cover of anyone's magazine. She won't be invited on *Oprah*. She'll live and die without much fanfare. But she's lived a very rich expression of the love of Christ. Her life may encourage you to pursue the dream God's placed in you.

I should admit that my own childhood, like many, had a

pitifully ignorant understanding of racial history in the South. I did note that the year our high school integrated, we suddenly had a winning football team. But I understood so little of the burdens we were all carrying from our shame-filled past. Jesse is one of many women God has used to open the eyes of my heart—and to show me how great his mercy flows.

On the day I visited Jesse, she had just moved into an apartment building for the elderly. Boxes of her belongings were everywhere. "Just clear off a spot, so we can sit and visit a while," she said, feeling no need to apologize or impress. Her story began to unfold.

"I grew up as the middle child of eleven children, born into a sharecropping family that worked from sunup to sundown," she began. Her father farmed another man's land—always someone else's land. Jesse's job as a small child was to pick the suckers off tomato plants. She had no more future ahead of her than her father, who worked his entire life and never had a square foot of land he could call his own.

So when Jesse turned eighteen, she caught a train for New York City. There she met a man who charmed the socks off her. After she married him, they moved back to North Carolina and lived with his parents. She bore him three children. It was a promising picture until this charming man proved he could not resist the attraction of other women.

By her early twenties, Jesse was on her own, raising two daughters and a son with no resources and no education. One of the best days in her life, she says, is when the first public-housing project opened up in Raleigh, right at the end of the war. "It was a place I could finally call home," Jesse explained. She loved waking up before dawn and taking a metal peg-leg tub onto the porch where she washed clothes by hand and hung them to dry. Then she'd pour herself a cup of coffee and watch the morning come, chatting with neighbors on their way to somewhere. This was her little place in the sun.

But the 1960s rolled in and, unfortunately, this picture changed, nearly overnight. Drugs swept through these communities, and neighborhoods became slums. Children wandered around hungry and alone, left to grow up by their own devices. So Jesse began to rise before dawn for a new reason. Morning and night, Jesse baked two dozen biscuits. Any child who was hungry was welcome at her table. Some days she could offer them meat. And always, there was blackstrap molasses. She became the neighborhood mother.

Jesse began an after-school program. In an effort to cut down on drug traffic, she rallied the city to establish a police station next door. Others came and left these projects, but Jesse stayed. She could have moved out numerous times, but Jesse felt the call of God to remain where she was. It was the door He had opened to her, and she felt a sense of purpose there.

Somewhere in our conversation, I asked Jesse how many children other than her own had she raised. "Oh, let's see . . . there was James and Yolanda and Tyrone and Bertie and . . ." —a roll call of little faces lining up in her memory, children now grown for whom Jesse was the dependable adult in their hard young lives.

Jesse is in her eighties now. The world's deep hunger is still there—it just takes a different shape. She has a new plan. Her next project is rounding up fabric and sewing machines so the older ladies in her building can piece together quilts for residents of a local nursing home.

Her parting comment was one that stuck with me for a long time. "God has been so good to me, sometimes I just have to pinch myself."[3]

## THE ROOT OF JOY

I am grateful for the women I've known through the years. Some wear real pearls and travel to exotic places. And others, like Jesse, have hardly left the place where they were born. But the common theme that emerges from the lives of women who smile at the future—women who love their lives—is that they've discovered the intersection where their deep gladness and the world's deep hunger meet.

A sense of purpose is meant to govern our lives. The apostle Paul said that he was always moving forward, pressing on, longing to "lay hold of that for which . . . [he] was laid hold of by Christ Jesus" (Phil. 3:12). We want to lay hold of the reason God laid hold of us—because there is a reason.

What I'm really saying is that our two dozen biscuits—offered in his name—make a difference. God takes what seems common and makes it extraordinary in his kingdom. We may live in a grand house on a hill—or be the daughter of a sharecropper. But our journey is really about finding these biscuits in one form or the other. You will know it when you do. It may not look momentous to anyone else, but you know it's right because there's joy there. Or as Madeline L'Engle writes in one of her poems:

> To grow up
> is to find
> the small part you are playing
> in this extraordinary drama
> written by
> somebody else.[4]

It is a small part you and I are called to play—but it's a small part in an incredible drama. And growing up is somehow about the courage to claim our part.

The fine irony is this: discovering that small part, the one with your name on it, is often the phoenix that rises from the ashes of your broken dreams. This truth caught me by surprise. We think of offering God our talents, but he is not in short supply. He is not all that impressed with our talent.

Rather, what God gives you to give the world often comes from your wounds and secret griefs. Like the friend of mine who counseled women considering abortion, these griefs become the passion that fuels your heart. They are the places where you hear God's voice. In some mysterious way, God redeems what's been lost and then transforms it into the cup of cold water you offer in his name. And that is, truly, better than your original dreams of the life you thought you wanted.

As I write this, I see the faces of women who've lived this reality. There's Marge, a fabric artist whose creations speak of the beauty and wholeness she discovered on the far side of debilitating depression. Or Debra, whose father died before she knew him. Her great joy is sponsoring a forgiveness ministry for prison inmates whose children get to visit them for the day. I think of Diana, who opened her home to Russian orphans after her husband's bike accident. Truly, some of the richest pleasures in life come from the gifts you give out of the understanding and empathy that pain has brought you.

> *The common theme that emerges from the lives of women who smile at the future—women who love their lives—is that they've discovered the intersection where their deep gladness and the world's deep hunger meet.*

Women who emerge from the pages of Scripture also speak of how God redeems and transforms broken dreams into good gifts. If we had known Rahab, whose name is always followed by her ignominy—Rahab, the harlot—would anyone have guessed that her courageous act of trusting the God of Israel for deliverance would take her from an empty existence as a prostitute . . . to a life of wife and mother (see Josh. 2:1–24; Matt. 1:1–17)? Yet her son Boaz is held up as the Old Testament paragon of a truly righteous man.

When I talk with a woman who can't see light in the tunnel of her life, I often ask her, "What brings you joy? What do you do that makes you secretly glad you were put on the planet for moments like this?" And when she responds that her life is so full of duty and obligation that she has stopped thinking in terms of what she enjoys, I know we are in trouble. When a woman gets weighed down with responsibilities, when hard things have happened . . . there's a great temptation to let go of the joy part. We stop looking for the biscuits we are put here to offer.

This is not the way Christ lived. Scripture makes clear that his hands were clasped around the nails that pinned him to a cross of suffering, but his eyes were focused on the joy.

> . . . fixing our eyes on Jesus, the author and perfecter of faith, who for the joy set before Him endured the cross, despising the shame . . . (Heb. 12:2)

Christ's joy was the redemption that would come from his great sacrifice. His life was not about *have to, ought to, should*—suffering for the sake of suffering. Christ's great pleasure was that he would bring us home to the Father.

That principle translates by small measures into our lives as well. For there is no joy quite like that of offering what you sense you are meant to give—whether that's creating beautiful table settings for a meeting or counseling women in distress or teaching a Bible study or having a hospitable home. Or like Jesse, fixing two dozen biscuits twice a day for children who need a mother. To simply walk out a journey with Christ and give out of whatever grief has been yours is to taste real joy.

## STARING DOWN YOUR INADEQUACY

The surprising thing about stepping into a spot prepared for you—or offering what you are meant to give—is that the sense of inadequacy never quite goes away. I have looked at other women who were living in their gifts and calling, and I have assumed their cups always brimmed over with confidence. If God pulled you into this, wouldn't your insecurities disappear?

I have come to think not. Those inadequacies are strangely persistent. Perhaps I can illustrate what I mean.

A few years back, I began to listen to the stories of women coming out of college into their first jobs or the early stages of a marriage. I heard a chronic refrain of regret—sexual regret—in their lives. The guys they'd slept with who haunted their dreams, the sense of something innocent and lovely lost they could not recover—their stories struck a note of grief in me. Often, I was the one reaching for a tissue. I came to wonder if I was feeling, essentially, the grief of God for women thrown into the sexual chaos of our day.

So I wrote on the topic.[5] And writing has an odd way of taking you into groups of people you would never meet. I found myself speaking to women on college campuses about sexuality and God. I have become the older woman, the therapist who can describe in detail the pain that comes on the heels of sleeping around. I get the opportunity to talk about the beauty God's invested in their souls . . . as women . . . and what it means to protect that.

But honestly, I have to stare down the same sense of inadequacy every single time I speak on the subject. A particular apparition appears in my head. I look out into a small sea of beautiful young faces (some are thrilled with the topic; others would throw a tomato if they had one) and always this thought comes forward: *I wonder how many of them are secretly thinking, "This woman is too old and too ugly to be a sexual being. Who brought her here to speak on this topic?"* That's what I read into their lovely faces.

> *The places where you feel less than competent are often strangely fused to your actual gifts and calling.*

This is not a terribly rational thought, I realize. But I have to step over it every time. It's the particular form my own inadequacy takes as it's projected onto these young women.

I mention this because I suspect I am not alone. The real truth I've come to believe is that gifting and inadequacy are Siamese twins joined at the hip. One is never quite without the other. The places where you feel less than competent are often strangely fused to your actual gifts and calling.

The apostle Paul, for all his apparent confidence, seems to hint at this very thing. He writes with a sense of awe that God leads us down a trail of victory in which the sweet aroma of Christ is emanating through us even when we are totally unaware of it. And then he adds, quite honestly:

> . . . And who is adequate for these things? . . . Not that we are adequate in ourselves to consider anything as coming

from ourselves, but *our adequacy is from God, who also made us adequate* as servants of a new covenant . . . (2 Cor. 2:16; 3:5–6; emphasis added)

Apparently, God delights in supplying what we are missing. Our inadequacy is not such an issue, really. Maybe it's more like an occasion and an opportunity for God to be God.

I know it's tempting to hold back on offering your two-dozen biscuits—waiting and waiting until this glowing sense of competency descends on you. But you can wait your life away. The way God grows us up inside is counter to what we expect. For as Søren Kierkegaard, the Danish philosopher who lived more than a century ago, insisted:

[We must] venture to act in accordance with the truth . . . venture right into the middle of actuality. Risk—and then God will truly come. . . . God sits and watches to see if there is one single person who will venture.[6]

We must "venture to act," Kierkegaard says. We are like Israelites who see the Jordan River part only as we get our toes wet. So you pray and ask God to tug your heart in the right direction. And then you let your feet and your checkbook and your energy follow. But there will always be risk—and you may forever feel inadequate.

This comforts me when I stand to speak on a subject like sex—one that tends to touch everyone's deepest nerve. I have stopped expecting the inadequacy to go away. Instead, I watch for moments and occasions when I just simply sense the Spirit of God present. He alone can open up the beauty and the potential in being a woman, created in his image. I can feel his pleasure as his name is spoken in this unlikely setting—though I admit it comes from the lips of a woman who, indeed, may not mirror the subject matter.

## WHOSE MEASURING STICK?

One of the things I so appreciate about a woman like Jesse is that her life calls me to be faithful. *Do what God puts in front of you and trust him with the outcome.* That's what I hear in her life. And that has been a hard lesson to learn.

Lots of us suffer from an inflated picture of what it means to live a life that matters. I know I have. You assume that if God is writing your story, then surely something great will come of it. It's like one of Lily Tomlin's stand-up comedy lines: I always thought I would grow up to be somebody, but I found I should have been more specific.

The real problem, I believe, is in what we are prone to call *great*. We look at the children Jesse Copeland touched through the years and see the profound impact. But I don't think it ever felt great to Jesse. She just answered the simple call of God to remain where she was and love children who came her way. She offered biscuits and a nurturing heart, and God did his work.

It's no different for us. The irony is that whatever our gifts are, they feel ordinary inside our own skin—like, what else is new? You encourage others because you love doing that. Or you study and teach because you love seeing the light come on in other people's eyes. Or you direct a corporate board with exemplary ethics because that's what is right. You do what you do because God has laid his hand on your life—and because you can. But it rarely feels special or extraordinary.

One of the best parts of discovering a journey with Christ out of the ruins of what you thought your life would look like is that you no longer have to weigh the results in terms of success or failure. You get a pass from weighing this out in terms of success and failure. Your accomplishments don't have to light up anyone's mar-

> *Do what God puts in front of you and trust him with the outcome.*

quee. You have only to find how your deep gladness is meant to touch the world's deep hunger and be there—because the love of Christ is too good to keep to yourself. It may not be a life anyone will call great. But if you are "playing to an Audience of One,"[7] it will be rich and real and true—and that's what counts.

The place where I write is a small room converted from a corner of our garage. It has one window and a door jammed shut from humidity, walls that are covered in the quotes I love, and books stuffed into every crevice. I share this space with tiny black bugs that love the humidity. It is a humble perch from which to write. But I say no to fifty other possibilities, and I come here because somewhere in my soul, I believe that my own biscuits to offer are . . . words.

On a good writing day, it feels as though the work I do is, somehow, worth something out there in the real world. And on a bad writing day, when no words come or the ones that do get thrown away, I go after the black bugs. There is a real art to this as well. I line their miniscule carcasses on my windowsill as trophies to a hard day. When my husband calls in the afternoon and asks how the writing has gone and I reply, "Well, it's been about an eight-bug day," he knows exactly what I mean.

There's an awful ordinariness that goes with any sort of gift or calling. It tests your motivation and strains your nerves. Or as Flannery O'Connor, author of some the last century's best Southern novels and a woman who died in her thirties from lupus, once wrote, "You do not do art the best you can for art's sake, but for the sake of returning to the invisible God your increasing talent *to use or not to use, as he sees fit*" (emphasis added).[8]

> *The irony is that whatever our gifts are, they feel ordinary inside our own skin.*

This is not just true with art; it's true with anything. Whatever comes of what we have to give is whatever God allows to happen. We just simply bring our gift, such as it is, to him.

The secret that brings enormous freedom is something hidden in the fine print, so to speak, in many places in the Bible. God doesn't really need us. He has given us a place in the kingdom of the Son he loves. He has promised to make his Son a light to the nations—the One before whom every knee will bow. Even if God had a need, he wouldn't tell us because he owns the cattle on a thousand hills, and it all belongs to him.

One day we will take our place in an innumerable throng around his throne, among people who do not look or speak or think like us. We will join hands with folks from every tongue and tribe and people and nation to sing his praise. Between now and then, we have only to live out our small part of an extraordinary drama that is his alone. It's a great work that God is doing. We get to come along for the ride, that's all.[9]

*Whatever comes of what we have to give is whatever God allows to happen.*

C. S. Lewis once said that his goal in life was simply to be found at his post when Christ returned. That is, indeed, where we need to be—right in that juncture where our deep gladness matches the world's deep need. We want to be found at our post and in our place, offering whatever biscuits we are meant to share.

Truly, it's the best part of the journey.

## INTERVIEWING YOUR BLISS

*For this I have been born, and for this*
*I have come into the world . . .*
—JOHN 18:37

Think, for a few moments, about things you quietly love to do. If someone could interview you in those moments, you would say, "Yes, when I'm doing that, I'm glad I was put on the planet for this." It might be loving on small children . . . or providing leadership for a floundering group . . . or expressing something artistically . . . or encouraging the discouraged. Others might not be drawn there, but for you, something comes alive in your heart in those times.

Pick any three memories where you recognize this sort of quiet joy was present. See if you can find the common themes and motivating aspects of those experiences.

Take a few minutes and write about each memory. What were you actually doing? (Pay special attention to the verbs you use to describe that activity.) What did you find particularly enjoyable in each experience? What would you want to repeat about it if you could?

Look back at each memory as you've written about it. Find some colored pens or markers and choose a color to circle these words:

\* adjectives that describe what was motivating or enjoyable about the activity;

\* verbs that describe what you were doing;

\* words that reveal why you'd want to do that again, in some form.

As you stand back and look at the big picture, what common themes do you see? If a close friend had written what you've written, what would you say to her? What kind of steps might you encourage her to take?

You probably have in your hand a pretty accurate snapshot of at least some aspect of your deep gladness and your best contribution. As you pray about it, what comes to mind as a possible arena of the world's deep need right around you where God intends your joy and contribution to make a difference?

However God leads us in the expression of our gifts, there will also be an element of sacrifice and hardship. How does the joy you experience somehow make that difficulty much more palatable?

*Chapter 10*

# JOURNEY WELL

## FELLOWSHIP WITH HIM IS THE PRIZE

*Some luck lies in not getting what you wanted
but getting what you have, which once you have it
you may be smart enough to see
is what you would have wanted had you known.*
—GARRISON KEILLOR

*He has showed you, O man, what is good.
And what does the LORD require of you?
To act justly and to love mercy
and to walk humbly with your God.*
—MICAH 6:8 NIV

*Some marriages are like candlewicks that require patience and* careful handling before the flame takes hold. A friend of mine, Sandy, would describe her marriage in those very terms. She and her husband really struggled in their early years together. The turnaround came when her husband was diagnosed with a low-grade form of cancer. This is their story, and it's a story you will want to hear.

Sandy marvels now at the irony of how battling a chronic

illness brought her marriage a closeness they had not found any other way. For ten years Sandy and her husband weathered this fight, and somewhere in it all, they learned how to talk and share and love like there was no tomorrow. The flame in their marriage burst forth. Sometimes when you don't know what the future holds, you start to cherish what you have right now. What they cherished was each other.

Sandy had always wanted to take ballroom dancing lessons. She nursed a secret longing to be twirled around the dance floor in a lovely dress in the arms of a man who knew his steps. Her husband realized he was not well enough to twirl anyone on a dance floor, but he was a gracious soul. One year for Christmas, he purchased a package of lessons so Sandy, at least, could enjoy the experience with an instructor.

She took her gift certificate and stored it in the back of her dresser drawer. *When summer comes, I'll take these dance lessons.* But summer came, and her mind was elsewhere. Her husband had developed sudden acute leukemia, and while the doctors would never admit the gravity of the situation, Sandy knew. Her nursing background told her the truth about what her eyes saw—her husband was going downhill by the day. He would not make it through this illness.

A couple of days before he died, Sandy leaned down and whispered a question in her husband's ear. "Do you know you're dying?" she asked him. He shook his head yes. He knew.

"You're going to get to dance before I do," she said.

He smiled at the thought of that. He knew exactly what she meant. And then he said a very tender thing.

Sandy's husband summoned what little strength he had at that point and whispered in response, "I'll save the first dance for you."

## THE JOURNEY IS A DANCE

This may be one of the more beautiful relationship stories I've been told in my time. But it's really more than that. For the truth is that this journey you're on is also a dance. Only it is God who wants to dance with you. He wants to take you out into life on his arm. That will pull you from every back alley where you've found life in anything but him. It will take you out of the safe places—and onto the dance floor of life, where anything can happen.

But in this dance, you'll come to know him. While it takes sometimes half a lifetime to grasp this—truly, the prize isn't the fulfillment of our dreams; it's the fellowship with him. He is, as the parable claims, the hidden treasure worth selling all we own to possess.

This treasure, this dance, is better than our original dreams because what we always wanted has a chance to come true. From the ashes of our expectations comes an intimacy with him—an actual pleasure in his company. *There's really Someone there.* Letting go of what we thought we needed and entering life as a journey, a dance with God, is a grace-filled rite of passage.

I love the way this is mirrored in the life of John, whose experience of the love of Christ was so real he could only describe himself as "the disciple whom Jesus loved." *If you want to know who I am, it's as simple as this: I am a man whom Jesus loves.* Don't we long to be able to ground our identity in the one thing we can never lose—that we are loved by God?

You may win awards and get fancy degrees with letters to put by your name. You may grow flowers that should grace the cover of *Southern Living.* Maybe your son will become a senator.

But the tables can also turn the other direction. You may never reach your goals. Your garden may become choked with weeds. Your children might grow up to disappoint you.

*The truth is that this journey you're on is also a dance.*

Neither picture—success or failure—is who you actually are if what really matters at the end of the day is this: *you are a woman whom Jesus loves.*

Even the apostle John did not wrap his heart around this reality by any easy route, though. John had his dreams too. Early on, he heard Jesus describe the suffering and the death that awaited him. John (and his brother James) skipped right past those words to the goal they had in mind: "Grant that we may sit one on Your right and one on Your left, in Your glory" (Mark 10:37). John wanted the first seat to the right of the One in power. He was a man with ambition and drive, a clear picture of the position he wanted to occupy.

This early snapshot of John is helpful to remember because we meet John again, as an old man on the island of Patmos.

He is living as an exile, away from all that felt like home. Listen to the words of a man who let go of his own dreams and who was changed by his journey with Christ. This is the way he describes himself: "I, John, your brother and companion in the suffering and kingdom and patient endurance that are ours in Jesus . . ." (Rev. 1:9 NIV).

> *Truly, the prize isn't the fulfillment of our dreams; it's the fellowship with him.*

You can almost hear John's voice. *Yes, there are some hard times . . . but, oh, there's a kingdom! And, of course, a measure of patient endurance is part of following Jesus.* John, who knew the richness of Christ's love, wanted us to realize that he saw himself as a companion on the same journey.

## WHO WILL YOU BECOME?

Posted on the wall just above the corner where I write, I keep a small copy of Paul Delarouche's famous painting of The Execution of Lady Jane Grey. It's set in an era of British history when wars were fought over matters of faith. Lady Jane Grey was a seventeen-year-old who chose to be beheaded rather than compromise what she believed.[1]

In the painting she stands blindfolded with a face as white as her dress, her ladies-in-waiting fainting in the background, a dispassionate executioner in red pants waiting to fulfill his task. In a stark and macabre way, the painting is beautiful.

I do have more pleasant subject matter gracing my walls, but I keep this picture close at hand. Without words, it speaks to me about the radical costliness of belonging to Christ. This journey with him is not a walk in the park. Christ is not a convenient addition to a life already crammed full of good stuff. Though I hope, quite literally, to keep my head on—I need to be reminded that this journey demands my life.

C. S. Lewis once noted that God's love is unique in the universe in that it consumes and yet leaves us more intact. That is a wonderful paradox. Perhaps you know instinctively what Lewis means. Much of what you once held dear and built your life on slowly crumbles and fades. Sometimes you actually watch it go up in smoke. What we clutch has a way of being pried from our grips. And yet God is there, shaping in you and through you what he really means to come of your life. This woman you are becoming, and will be in Christ for all eternity, is more real and more alive. The love of God does consume—and yet the real you emerges, strangely more intact.

What kind of shape is this process taking in your life? Who are you becoming? Are you a contemporary version of Mary Magdalene, delivered from a painful past—a woman whose forgiveness gives her the faithfulness to remain when everyone else flees?

Or are you a modern Lydia? You know how to dress in the best purple fabrics, and perhaps the hors d'oeuvres that grace your table are catered. You hold a few key positions in town. Yet you often steal away—as Lydia did in Philippi—to meet with others outside the city so that you can hear more about the One who has touched your life so deeply.

Perhaps, you will become a present-day version of Deborah, a woman able to rise above your culture to speak words that silence other's doubts and challenge them to faith and courage.

I do not know what shape this *becoming* will take in you— only that it never ends and that it's worth the price you pay. I believe that something will come of our lives that is truly better than our dreams—and that God will get the glory in that. It's not an easy path, but it's the only journey worth taking.

## BECOMING GRATEFUL

People who have let go of their expectations of how they think life is supposed to look usually stumble upon gratitude—which is a wonderful thing to find. You stop waiting for life to begin when it's fixed and all the broken parts are healed. It's now, in *this* moment, *this* conversation, *this* sunset.

Picture this scene with me because you have many just like it. It's a warm spring day, and I have too much to do. But I'm sitting outside a bagel shop under Bartlett pear trees in bloom, with my daughter and the son she prayed for. Andrew is making a mess with his cream cheese, half of which now graces his cheeks in white smudges. He waves at every car that passes—surely, these people have come just to see him. He is a prince holding court.

In the past, when my focus was about trying to get God to do with my life what I thought he needed to do, I would have totally missed such a moment. I would have been mentally clicking through my to-do list, moving on to the next thing—or preoccupied by the parts of my life that were not going well.

To be on a journey with the Lord is to have the freedom to savor what he brings your way—and to see it all as a gift. It's like a Monopoly game where you get your two hundred dollars for passing "Go," but you don't have to waste away in the jail of this-should-have-been and I-wish-it-were. The truth is that there will always be something missing in the picture. Gratitude is getting to enjoy the moment under the pear tree—even though you (like me) may well have a husband who travels a great deal and a lonely, aging mother and a friend with cancer.

Moments like these are everywhere around you, but gratitude allows you to take them in. Gratitude is what keeps you from standing knee-deep in a river of water and dying of thirst.

I don't want to live like my sweet Aunt Minnie, who when she died, still had all her monogrammed towels in her hope chest—unused, as fresh as the wedding day on which they were given fifty years before. I want to live lavishly the life that God has set before me, trusting his glory to peek through the torn edges. I want to go for broke.

I write this, knowing well there are aspects of your life—and of mine—that we'd both give our eyeteeth to change. Difficult personalities usually remain difficult, and sometimes they are right in your backyard and you can't move across the country. I think of my husband's ministry, which is always blazing a new trail—and I much prefer the sure and certain. Or maybe it's a battle with depression that keeps you measuring how far you are from a black hole that never quite goes away.

Whatever it is, it's there for all of us. It's what I call *a chosen ache*—meaning not that I'd choose it, but I'm making choices to accept its presence as something God has allowed for his own reasons—which must be good ones because He is good.

If my fairy tale had come true—some crazy version of the big house on the hill and children in smocked clothing—I suspect I would have been lost in a nightmare, rather than a dream. Knowing my own weaknesses, I fear that Christ might be little more than a charm on my silver bracelet—which is to say, I am as grateful for what God has withheld as for what he's given.

If I'm honest, I see with irony that my own chosen aches are the very places where Christ has become real for me. I may have been pulled there kicking and screaming, but this is where his

> *To be on a journey with the Lord is to have the freedom to savor what he brings your way—and to see it all as a gift.*

forgiveness and love and power actually captured my heart. I see the wisdom of the aches God has chosen to leave in the story. More and more, a little refrain beats in the background of my mind: *God knows what he's doing with your life. He knows what he's doing. He knows . . .*

It's interesting that if you read the book of Hebrews, you

will follow a trail of *better thans*. Christ is better than the angels and the prophets and the priests—and all that came before. You will emerge near the end of the book to one great *therefore*.

Considering the majesty and wonder of this God who became flesh and who invites us to be at home in his kingdom . . . how do we respond? The writer of Hebrews answers simply:

> Therefore, since we receive a kingdom which cannot be shaken, *let us show gratitude,* by which we may offer to God an acceptable service with reverence and awe. (12:28; emphasis added)

## THE ESSENCE OF HOPE

Perhaps you read about the woman in Proverbs 31 who bought and sold, cooked and sewed, whose lamp never went out at night—and like me, your first impulse is to reach for your vitamins. Of all the virtues of this woman, though, there is one descriptor I cherish above all. If I could pick any phrase that I prayed would be true of my life, it would be this one: "Strength and dignity are her clothing, *And she smiles at the future*" (v. 25, emphasis added).

If you have traveled far at all in this journey with the Lord, you know the significance of that phrase—to smile at the future. How do you do that when you are staring in the face of what's been lost along the way? How do you look with hope to the future, if the present is vastly different than you anticipated?

The story of most women's lives is the story of our attachments to people we love. And yet children grow up and friends change and, in the end, everyone dies. What's to smile at, humanly speaking? It's no wonder, really, that alcoholism is such a problem for women over sixty, as women start to tally their losses. And those losses are there to tally.

I believe that smiling at the future starts way back on the journey. It's a habit of heart you cultivate every time your present reality disappoints—and you are comforted in the presence of the Lord. Smiling at the future is possible if it holds all you've longed for. Your faith is not a story you made up so you could sleep better at night. *The fairy tale does come true.* It's just not now. Not here. And not yet.

So we smile . . . because God always has more to this story. We live in hope because whatever tragedy strikes, it cannot usurp the blessing of God on our lives as we walk with him.

Many women's stories have helped me grow in this habit of the heart. I draw courage from their determination to trust God in the face of whatever. I watched a friend struggle for years in her husband's battle to be free of pornography—in the end, he succumbed, leaving her in a financial mess with children to raise. How can she smile at the future—I mean, really? Yet on her better days, she does. She gets up early in the morning because she craves a few moments of quiet with God. It sustains her. And as she sits there with him, she says, "Lord, you know where I am. You know what a long, hard road this has been. Would you surprise me with your goodness?"

I have adopted her phrase for those times in my life when the fog rolls in and all I know is that I will see God's goodness on the road ahead—somehow, in some way. *Yes, Lord, surprise me with your goodness. And let your glory be seen in this.*

> The fairy tale does come true. *It's just not now. Not here. And not yet.*

What we are counting on is the infinite capacity of God to redeem—not just our souls but the very broken pieces of living in a world where no one and nothing is as it was meant to be. We are banking on the goodness of God that never stops appearing in our story. We live the words of David all our days:

> I would have despaired unless I had believed that I would
> see the goodness of the LORD
> In the land of the living. (Ps. 27:13)

*It's quite a journey we embark upon, on the far side of our* dreams. Truly, it leads to places we did not intend to visit. God takes us down some narrow paths, full of briars and thorns. Would we come, by any easy route, to those broad, open spaces where his grace is poured out through our cracked pots into the lives of others? Would we find our dancing shoes any other way?

These days, having journeyed now a while, my favorite form of smiling at the future takes place in our cul-de-sac on clear nights beneath tall Carolina pine trees. If the moon is out, that's where my grandson, Andrew, wants to be. He is fascinated by the moon. "Oh, wow," he says, as he cups two toddler hands around his dirty little cheeks. "Oh, wow." And then he blows the moon a kiss.

So when there's a big moon rising, I grab my iPod and we head outdoors. I put one earpiece in his ear and one in mine— and off we go, dancing in the moonlight. Sometimes I want to freeze the moment. *Does it get any better than this?* I wonder.

If I read the Story right, I believe it gets much better than this—better than our wildest dreams. This journey that you and I are on actually leads somewhere. It is whispered that one day, we will dance with the King.

And for once, we won't have to worry about finding the right dress to wear.

# REFLECTION AND STUDY GUIDE

## USING THIS SECTION OF THE BOOK

As I wrote the study section for this book, I pictured myself sitting down with you over a cup of coffee with the time and space to think about what has happened in your own journey with the Lord. My hope is that this will serve as a guide in that process, whether used individually or in a small-group setting.

You will find that the verses have been printed out and that, in most cases, they are from the New American Standard Bible (NASB), simply because the wording in that version is so beautiful and powerful. Feel free to look them up in a translation you prefer.

Certainly, the lasting changes in my life have usually come about through the *holy trio* of studying Scripture, talking with others, and journaling that tills up the soil of my own heart. I hope these questions will help that process along in you—and that you will feel the freedom to write about what God brings to mind without too much analyzing or critique. The best journaling simply unearths what you can then pray about. What we trust is not the process but the reality of God, who has promised to complete the good work he began in us when we first came to know him. He is the One who takes us by the hand through the terrain of our own hearts so that we emerge more secure in his love—more able to offer that love to others.

My prayer is that you will emerge a few steps further down the path with a strength and graciousness of spirit that comes from tasting more of the love of Jesus—which, as the old hymn says, is "love of every love the best."

—Paula Rinehart

*Chapter 1*

# A DIFFERENT KIND OF WONDERFUL

1. How has the video of your life played out differently than you originally hoped it would—or thought it should?

What part of this *wonderful plan for your life* did you not expect?

2. Write and/or talk about one time in your life when you might have echoed the question, "Why is God holding out on me?" Is there a *good dream* for which God seems to have said *no* or *wait*?

3. I've noticed that in those times when I get bogged down in my own story—my patchwork quilt—the majesty and greatness of God is often antidotal.

Read this incredible passage from Isaiah 40, and let it lift you out of the question of what has happened or not happened in your life:

Do you not know? Have you not heard?
Has it not been declared to you from the beginning?
Have you not understood from the foundations
    of the earth?
It is He who sits above the circle of the earth,
And its inhabitants are like grasshoppers,
Who stretches out the heavens like a curtain
And spreads them out like a tent to dwell in.
He it is who reduces rulers to nothing,
Who makes the judges of the earth meaningless.
Scarcely have they been planted,
Scarcely have they been sown,
Scarcely has their stock taken root in the earth,
But He merely blows on them, and they wither,
And the storm carries them away like stubble.
"To whom then will you liken Me
That I would be his equal?" says the Holy One.
Lift up your eyes on high
And see who has created these stars,
The One who leads forth their host by number,
He calls them all by name;
Because of the greatness of His might and
    the strength of His power
Not one of them is missing.

Why do you say, O Jacob, and assert, O Israel,
"My way is hidden from the LORD,
And the justice due me escapes the notice of my God"?
Do you not know? Have you not heard?
The Everlasting God, the LORD, the Creator of
     the ends of the earth
Does not become weary or tired
His understanding is inscrutable.
He gives strength to the weary,
And to him who lacks might He increases power.
Though youths grow weary and tired,
And vigorous young men stumble badly,
Yet those who wait for the LORD
Will gain new strength;
They will mount up with wings like eagles,
They will run and not get tired,
They will walk and not become weary.
(Isa. 40:21–31)

As you read these verses, what reminds you of God's majesty and brings a sense of awe? How do these verses speak to you?

4. King David, who could genuinely have about anything he wanted, asked God to save him from an attitude of entitlement.

Listen to his words from Psalm 19:13: "Also keep back Your servant from presumptuous sins; let them not rule over me; then I will be blameless, and I shall be acquitted of great transgression."

How do you think presumption and entitlement in our lives lead us into greater difficulties and bigger mistakes?

5. Christ is our pattern and example in all things. What do you hear in this description of Christ's life in Hebrews 2:9–10? What does this mean for our lives?

But we do see Him who was made for a little while lower than the angels, namely, Jesus, because of the suffering of death crowned with glory and honor, so that by the grace of God He might taste death for everyone. For it was fitting for Him, for whom are all things, and through whom are all things, in bringing many sons to glory, to perfect the author of their salvation through sufferings.

6. What do the following verses say about God's purpose for your life, and how does this reality encourage you?

Now the God of peace, who brought up from the dead the great Shepherd of the sheep through the blood of the eternal covenant, even Jesus our Lord, equip you in every good thing to do His will, working in us that which is pleasing in His sight, through Jesus Christ, to whom be the glory forever and ever. (Heb. 13:20–21)

7. How can a person be a Christian for years and still say, "I feel like I'm just beginning to know God"?

Are you starting to know God in ways that feel new and fresh and like something you have waited on for a long time? How is that happening?

8. Brennan Manning, in some of his lectures and books, quotes the benediction of an old priest, Larry Hines. The benediction goes as follows:

May all your expectations be frustrated;

May all your plans be thwarted.

May all your desires be withered into nothingness

So that you may experience the poverty and
    powerlessness of a child . . .

And sing and dance in the great compassionate heart
    of God.[1]

What do you think he means? What draws you in this benediction?

9. As you consider the patchwork quilt of your life, describe some of the moments when you experienced a stirring of God's *wild hope.*

# Chapter 2

# THE DANGER OF SETTLING

1. Perhaps from time to time, it's not great expectations that afflict you—but *hoping for too little*. How does that happen in your life?

    What is the danger of not hoping, not wanting . . . just settling?

2. What's your personal brand of squelching a hope or a dream? Check all that apply:

    \_\_\_\_ calling it *selfish*

    \_\_\_\_ deciding it's too painful to hope for what may not happen

    \_\_\_\_ pretending you don't have a dream

    \_\_\_\_ staying too anxious or fearful to feel your longing

    \_\_\_\_ other:

How do you feel about that?

3. One particular story in the Gospels is the account of a man named Bartimaeus, whose hope or dream was obvious—Bartimaeus was blind. He sat by the road to Jericho day after day, seeking alms. One day he heard that Jesus was passing by, and Bartimaeus was not about to miss his one opportunity. "Son of David, have mercy on me!" he cried out, even when others scolded him. And Jesus stopped, looked right at his blindness, and asked him the question of his life.

As you read his story in Mark 10:46–52, let yourself *become* Bartimaeus. You have a need, a longing, a great desire.

> Then they came to Jericho. And as He was leaving Jericho with His disciples and a large crowd, a blind beggar named Bartimaeus, the son of Timaeus, was sitting by the road. When he heard that it was Jesus the Nazarene, he began to cry out and say, "Jesus, Son of David, have mercy on me!" Many were sternly telling him to be quiet, but he kept crying out all the more, "Son of David, have mercy on me!" And Jesus stopped and said, "Call him here." So they called the blind man, saying to him, "Take courage, stand up! He is calling for you." Throwing aside his cloak, he jumped up, and came to Jesus. And answering him, Jesus said, "What do you want Me to do for you?" And the blind man said to Him, "Rabboni, I want to regain my sight!" And Jesus said to him, "Go; your faith has made you well." Immediately he regained his sight and began following Him on the road.

How do you feel when Jesus asks you the same question?

How do you respond?

What about this story quickens your hope?

4. What is your usual approach to managing disappointment on your own?

In those seasons, how would you describe your caricature of God?

5. The really important part is where we go with an aching heart. Where have you gone in times past that you regret?

6. I find the book of Isaiah to be an unfathomable source of comfort and support when my own heart is in need of repair. The prophet's words in Isaiah 61:1–3 are also the first words Christ chose to speak when he began his public ministry (see Luke 4:18–19). These words are filled with promise and hope.

> The Spirit of the Lord GOD is upon me,
> Because the LORD has anointed me
> To bring good news to the afflicted;
> He has sent me to bind up the brokenhearted,
> To proclaim liberty to captives,
> And freedom to prisoners;
> To proclaim the favorable year of the LORD
> And the day of vengeance of our God;
> To comfort all who mourn,
> To grant those who mourn in Zion,
> Giving them a garland instead of ashes,
> The oil of gladness instead of mourning,
> The mantle of praise instead of a spirit of fainting.
> So they will be called oaks of righteousness,
> The planting of the LORD, that He may be glorified.

How do these verses speak to you? If you could believe these promises more deeply, how would they help you hold on to hope?

7. What do you see of yourself in Hannah and Naomi?

What touches you the most in their stories?

8. The apostle Peter makes a startling claim, spoken in the context of suffering and difficulty, and quoted originally from Isaiah.

He says, simply, "Behold I lay in Zion a choice stone, a precious corner stone, and he who believes in Him will not be disappointed" (1 Pet. 2:6).

From what you've experienced of life, what do you think Peter is actually saying?

How would that be translated into your own experience?

# Chapter 3

# DISTURBING INTERRUPTIONS

1. What qualifies as a *disturbing interruption* in your life?

2. In what ways have you sensed that God is in the process of saving you from yourself?

3. The Danish philosopher Søren Kierkegaard once said that it sometimes seems as though God is deceiving us because, in the beginning, we believe that "God will love us according to our idea of love."[2] Do you identify with his comment?

In what ways do you see that God's love is, indeed, different from human love?

4. Hebrews 12:5–11 is a classic passage that allows us to see the love of God in the midst of challenges we would not normally welcome:

You have forgotten the exhortation which is addressed to you as sons,

"My son, do not regard lightly the discipline of the LORD,
Nor faint when you are reproved by Him;
For those whom the LORD loves He disciplines,
And He scourges every son whom He receives."

It is for discipline that you endure; God deals with you as with sons; for what son is there whom his father does not discipline? But if you are without discipline, of which all have become partakers, then you are illegitimate children and not sons. Furthermore, we had earthly fathers to discipline us, and we respected them; shall we not much rather be subject to the Father of spirits, and live? For they disciplined us for a short time as seemed best to them, but He disciplines us for our good, so that we may share His holiness. All discipline for the moment seems not to be joyful, but sorrowful; yet to those who have been trained by it, afterwards it yields the peaceful fruit of righteousness.

How would you apply this passage to something currently in your life that you wish wasn't there?

5. God is at work in your life through the disturbing interruptions you mentioned above. What kinds of dependencies or old ways of coping are being challenged in your life?

In what ways might God be *springing the lock* on your heart and soul?

6. Disillusionment is often a great grace in our lives because there are illusions that, indeed, we need to let go of. What are some of the illusions and lies about yourself, about others—about God—that God has revealed to you in the last five years? What freedom has that brought in your life?

7. Think of other seasons in your life when the unexpected has happened or the bottom has dropped out in some way—and you sought God in that time. What is yours—what do you own—because of what God gave or taught you during that season?

8. I mentioned that some difficulties remain and that an invisible pendulum in us swings between "Lord, please take this away!" and "Will I let God transform me in this?" Where is that pendulum in your inner life?

What would it look and feel like to allow the difficulty that remains to be what God uses to shape something of beauty through which his glory shines . . . through you?

*Chapter 4*

# OWNING YOUR STUFF

1. Think about a moment of insight or a season of revelation when God showed you something about yourself you had not seen before—or had not been able to face honestly. In what ways did you sense his kindness and his mercy in that new revelation?

2. I wrote about a season in my own life when I realized I was being seduced by a philosophy that seemed to promise something more attractive than Christ. Is there anything or anyone in your life that causes you to feel that kind of pull?

What does that attraction appear to offer you?

How would you journal and pray about the pull you are experiencing—or perhaps experienced in the past?

3. The middle chapters of the book of Isaiah are falling out of my Bible from years of returning to them. One verse describes with startling accuracy what happens in our lives when anything or anyone other than God is more central or too important to us.

Isaiah says that when something is idolatrous in our lives, our hearts feed on ashes and, over time, we can become so deceived we can't see what is happening. Here is Isaiah's picture of self-deception:

> They do not know, nor do they understand, for He has smeared over their eyes so that they cannot see and their hearts so that they cannot comprehend. . . . He feeds on ashes; a deceived heart has turned him aside. And he cannot deliver himself, nor say, "Is there not a lie in my right hand?" (Isa. 44:18–20)

The verses below are God's remedy for our self-deception. What do these verses say to you about the heart of God, his longing for you, and his claim upon your life?

"Remember these things, O Jacob,

And Israel, for you are My servant;

I have formed you, you are My servant,

O Israel, you will not be forgotten by Me.

I have wiped out your transgressions like a thick cloud,

And your sins like a heavy mist

Return to Me, for I have redeemed you."

Shout for joy, O heavens, for the LORD has done it!

Shout joyfully, you lower parts of the earth;

Break forth into a shout of joy, you mountains,

O forest, and every tree in it;

For the LORD has redeemed Jacob

And in Israel He shows forth His glory.

(Isa. 44:21–23)

4. *There are parts of me that have never heard the gospel.* What does that statement mean in your life?

5. Read Ephesians 3:14–19 in light of what you've written.

For this reason, I bow my knees before the Father, from whom every family in heaven and on earth derives its name, that He would grant you, according to the riches of His glory, to be strengthened with power through His Spirit in the inner man, so that Christ may dwell in your hearts through faith; and that you, being rooted and grounded in love, may be able to comprehend with all the saints what is the breadth and length and height and depth, and to know the love of Christ which surpasses knowledge, that you may be filled up to all the fullness of God.

What is the hope you feel as you read these verses?

6. Do you agree with Brennan Manning's insight that, as women, we are often held back in our relationship with God by our own self-condemnation?

How is this true in your own life—or not?

7. Psalm 40 offers a beautiful picture of what an actual change of heart looks like.

Sacrifice and meal offering You have not desired;
My ears You have opened;
Burnt offering and sin offering You have not required.
Then I said, "Behold, I come;
In the scroll of the book it is written of me;
I delight to do Your will, O my God;
Your Law is within my heart. (vv. 6–8)

How would you write these verses in your own words?

8. If you think of something in your life that represents bondage or defeat, what would concrete steps of change look like for you? As you pray about it, what comes to your mind as the next needed step?

*Therefore, strengthen the hands that are weak*
*and the knees that are feeble,*
*and make straight paths for your feet,*
*so that the limb which is lame*
*may not be put out of joint, but rather be healed.*
(Heb. 12:12–13)

# Chapter 5

# GROWING UP TOGETHER

1. The apostle John wrote, "If we walk in the light, as he is in the light, we have fellowship with one another, and the blood of Jesus, his Son, purifies us from all sin" (1 John 1:7 NIV). What does it mean—or what would it mean—for you to walk in the light with at least a few others?

2. Describe a relationship in which another person knows you in your weakness and failure—as well as your better moments.

What kind of impact has that relationship had on your life and walk with God?

3. When you think about your fears and reservations about allowing others to know you (the good, the bad, and the ugly), which of these statements apply?

    \_\_\_ I'm convinced that others won't like what they see.
    \_\_\_ I think my stuff is worse than other people's stuff.
    \_\_\_ I've had some bad experiences (rejection, nonacceptance) that I haven't gotten over.
    \_\_\_ I don't quite see the point in all this.

In what ways do your fears and reservations keep you from loving others well?

4. I wrote about a close friend who challenged me when she thought I was heading in the wrong direction. Have you experienced this level of honesty with someone?

How did this honesty impact your life—or theirs?

5. Read Romans 15:5–7.

> Now may the God who gives perseverance and encourage-
> ment grant you to be of the same mind with one another
> according to Christ Jesus, so that with one accord you may
> with one voice glorify the God and Father of our Lord Jesus
> Christ. Therefore, accept one another, just as Christ also
> accepted us to the glory of God.

When have you experienced the love and acceptance and
mercy of God as it came to you through another?

Now picture a relationship in your life that feels challenging and at times, difficult. What would it look like to
mirror the love and acceptance and mercy of God to that
person?

6. First Peter 5:5 says, "All of you, clothe yourselves with
humility toward one another, for God is opposed to the proud,
but gives grace to the humble."

How do you experience the gentle nudging of God as you apply this verse to your closest relationships?

7. Philosopher Francis Schaeffer once noted that it is nearly impossible, humanly speaking, to strike the right balance between kindness and truth. He said only the Spirit of God can bring the right measure appropriately to bear in the moment.[3] In our own strength, we tend to either be kind at the expense of truth—or we tell the truth at the cost of kindness. "Speaking the truth in love," as Paul writes in Ephesians 4:15, is not often easy.

Which side—truth or kindness—are you more comfortable expressing in relationships?

What would it mean to let God lead you into a stronger expression of the one you tend to leave behind?

8. If God would give you more or less of any one thing as you seek to love others well and to experience the fellowship of other Christians more deeply, what would that be . . . and why would you want that?

*Do not let kindness and truth leave you;*
*Bind them around your neck,*
*Write them on the tablet of your heart.*
*So you will find favor and good repute*
*In the sight of God and man.* (Prov. 3:3–4)

# Chapter 6

# COMING IN SECOND

1. When and in what ways do you sometimes live as though it all depends on you?

How do you feel in those times?

2. When you think you absolutely must find the right path—the perfect choice—what is your fear? What are you afraid might happen if you simply pray, trust God, and step out in faith?

3. Many verses in Scripture speak of God's awesome majesty and his sovereign purposes. Here are three classic ones:

> But the plans of the LORD stand firm forever,
>> the purposes of his heart through all generations.
>> (Ps. 33:11 NIV)

I know that everything God does will endure forever; nothing
can be added to it and nothing taken from it. (Eccl. 3:14 NIV)

I make known the end from the beginning, from ancient
times, what is still to come. I say: My purpose will stand, and
I will do all that I please. (Isa. 46:10 NIV)

What comfort—and challenge—do you find in these verses?

4. I have been amazed to realize that Isaiah records the inner
life of Jesus as he faced the Cross. He took refuge and comfort in his Father's good and sovereign purposes.
Read and ponder Isaiah 50:4–9.

The Sovereign LORD has given me an instructed tongue,
    to know the word that sustains the weary.
He wakens me morning by morning,
    wakens my ear to listen like one being taught.
The Sovereign LORD has opened my ears,
    and I have not been rebellious;
    I have not drawn back.
I offered my back to those who beat me,
    my cheeks to those who pulled out my beard;
I did not hide my face
    from mocking and spitting.

Because the Sovereign Lord helps me,
> I will not be disgraced.

Therefore have I set my face like flint,
> and I know I will not be put to shame.

He who vindicates me is near.
> Who then will bring charges against me?
> Let us face each other!

Who is my accuser?
> Let him confront me!

It is the Sovereign Lord who helps me.
> Who is he that will condemn me?

They will all wear out like a garment;
> the moths will eat them up. (NIV)

What touches you in these verses? What would it mean for you to feel sustained by God in a similar way during your difficult moments?

5. Think of one personal regret or one thing in your life you wish had turned out differently. If it's true that God never wastes an experience on us, in what ways has God used this experience for good and for his glory?

6. The early church fathers considered despair to be sin because we know the end of the story—personally and for all time—is assured. *Our God reigns.* Why do you think they thought of hopelessness or despair . . . as sin?

7. Here are two verses in the New Testament that speak especially clearly of God's good purposes for our lives in him, prepared from all eternity.

> For I am confident of this very thing, that He who began a good work in you will perfect it until the day of Christ Jesus. (Phil. 1:6)

> For we are His workmanship, created in Christ Jesus for good works, which God prepared beforehand, so that we would walk in them. (Eph. 2:10)

How do these verses speak hope to you?

8. How would you see your story differently if you saw it through the lens of God's sovereignty?

What would it mean to lean your life more fully on that spiritual reality?

# Chapter 7

# THE EMPATHY OF JESUS

1. When do you experience the longing for someone to understand you—to feel what you feel from the inside out? What do you experience when they don't?

2. As a younger man, David had to hide in caves in order to escape Saul's efforts to hunt him down. A number of psalms record his experience, which often matches our own in moments when we feel truly alone.

When have you felt some aspect of what David records here in Psalm 142?

> I cry aloud to the LORD;
>> I lift up my voice to the LORD for mercy.
>
> When my spirit grows faint within me,
>> it is you who know my way . . .
> Look to my right and see;
>> no one is concerned for me.
> I have no refuge;
>> no one cares for my life. (vv. 1, 3–4 NIV)

Now look at what David does with what he's feeling. A few verses later, he writes:

I cry to you, O LORD;
    I say, "You are my refuge,
    my portion in the land of the living."
Listen to my cry,
    for I am in desperate need; . . .
Set me free from my prison,
    that I may praise your name. (vv. 5–7 NIV)

What thoughts comfort David in these moments? How would you put these last four lines in your own words?

3. Think of a situation in which you felt loss or betrayal or abandonment or fear. What would it mean to take in the reality that Christ understands—Christ has lived your experience?

4. I wrote about the way a sense of entitlement (believing one's life should be free of real hardship) can steal from us an awareness of experiencing God's presence with us.

The following verses (and dozens more) speak to our need

to accept suffering as a part of following Christ. What phrases stand out to you?

> For to you it has been granted for Christ's sake, not only to believe in Him, but also to suffer for His sake.
> (Phil. 1:29)

> For you have been called for this purpose, since Christ also suffered for you, leaving you an example for you to follow in His steps, who committed no sin, nor was any deceit found in His mouth; and while being reviled, He did not revile in return; while suffering, He uttered no threats, but kept entrusting Himself to Him who judges righteously; and He Himself bore our sins in His body on the cross, so that we might die to sin and live to righteousness; for by His wounds you were healed. (1 Pet. 2:21–24)

5. The apostle Paul wrote that his goal in life was "[to know Christ] and the power of His resurrection and the fellowship of His sufferings" (Phil. 3:10).

How do you think that walking with God through a hard time in your life can result in the fellowship of a deepening friendship with Christ?

6. One of the most familiar verses in Scripture is Psalm 23:4, which says, "Even though I walk through the valley of the shadow of death, I fear no evil; for You are with me."

The presence of a shadow in the valley of death can only mean that Christ is there, present as the Light. Even *there*, Christ is present.

How does this reality influence the way you look at your life?

7. One of my most favorite verses in Isaiah speaks of God's presence with us. It's a verse worth carrying through your days. I leave it with you as a sort of benediction on this topic:

"Do not fear, for I am with you;
Do not anxiously look about you, for I am your God.
I will strengthen you, surely I will help you,
Surely I will uphold you with My righteous right hand."
(Isa. 41:10)

If this verse could be set in concrete inside you, how would your life be different?

# Chapter 8

# LOVING (DIFFICULT) PEOPLE

1. What is *difficult* about your more difficult relationships or friendships?

2. What fear or insecurity or unmet need is unearthed in you in these relationships?

3. I mentioned that difficult relationships are one of the main ways God reaches into our hearts and frees us from having to have the stamp of human approval. How do you see it's possible for a difficult relationship to be the gymnasium of one's soul?

What sort of new strength or freedom do you sense God longs to give you through this unlikely means?

4. What we might call being a people-pleaser is what Scripture calls "the fear of man." When our lives are controlled by the fear of man, we can't love others well because we are paralyzed by our own fear of rejection. Isaiah records profound insights on this topic. Let's look at two, in particular.

In Isaiah 2, he writes about how men will hide in caves and holes in the ground in the great day of the Lord. They will throw away everything they've trusted instead of God. They will ask the rocks to cover them from "the terror of the LORD and the splendor of His majesty" (v. 21).

So Isaiah concludes with these words:

Stop regarding man, whose breath of life is in his nostrils;
For why should he be esteemed? (v. 22)

Then later in Isaiah, God says even more clearly:

"I, even I, am He who comforts you
Who are you that you are afraid of man who dies
And of the son of man who is made like grass." (Isa. 51:12)

What do you hear God saying through Isaiah about the fear of man and the excessive effort to please people in your own life?

5. From the list below, pick whichever phrase you need most and write about what its application would look like in your life:

The grace to hold lightly someone you love . . .

The courage to love someone boldly . . .

The humility to accept another person where
    they are in life . . .

6. Often the most important aspect of loving others well is realizing that your own love is insufficient and you need God's love poured through you. Pick a phrase in each of these verses that most captures how you would long for God's love to be poured through you.

Why did you choose the phrases you chose? (You can use these verses as a basis for prayer.)

To sum up, all of you be harmonious, sympathetic, brotherly, kindhearted, and humble in spirit; not returning evil for evil, or insult for insult, but giving a blessing instead; for you were called for the very purpose that you might inherit a blessing. (1 Pet. 3:8–9)

So, as those who have been chosen of God, holy and beloved, put on a heart of compassion, kindness, humility, gentleness and patience; bearing with one another, and forgiving each other, whoever has a complaint against anyone; just as the Lord forgave you, so also should you. (Col. 3:12–13)

"But love your enemies, and do good, and lend, expecting nothing in return; and your reward will be great, and you will be sons of the Most High; for He Himself is kind to ungrateful and evil men. Be merciful, just as your Father is merciful. Do not judge and you will not be judged; and do not condemn, and you will not be condemned; pardon, and you will be pardoned. Give, and it will be given to you. They will pour into your lap a good measure—pressed down, shaken together, and running over. For by your standard of measure it will be measured to you in return." (Luke 6:35–38)

7. Richard Rohr, a spiritual director who writes and speaks about God's transforming love, claims there is a basic litmus test of how far along we are in our journey of learning to love as Christ loved. He says that we will know God has done a deep work in our hearts when:

. . . we are no longer blaming anyone for our life;

. . . we are no longer looking for someone (to validate us).[4]

What kind of deep work is God doing in you as you seek to love as he loves?

8. Philosopher Francis Schaeffer wrote in his classic book *The Mark of a Christian* these words: "Love . . . is the mark Christ gave Christians to *wear* before the world. Only with this mark may the world know that Christians are indeed Christians and that Jesus was sent by the Father."

Schaeffer is drawing upon Christ's own words:

> "A new commandment I give to you, that you love one another, even as I have loved you, that you also love one another. By this all men will know that you are My disciples, if you have love for one another." (John 13:34–35)

In the relationship(s) you find difficult, how would others know that you belong to Christ?

*Chapter 9*

# THE PLACE MEANT FOR YOU

1. What part of the world's deep hunger are you most sensitive to—where does your heart become engaged?

If the obstacles in the path were removed and God allowed you to touch that need in some way . . . how would you most long to see the love and truth of Christ touch the world's deep needs through you?

2. When do you most experience that sense of doing something you were born for?

3. In what ways have you seen your own secret grief translated into *the biscuits* that you suspect you're meant to offer others in his name?

4. The apostle Paul writes about God as the One "who comforts us in all our troubles, so that we can comfort those in any trouble with the comfort we ourselves have received from God" (2 Cor. 1:4 NIV).

How has this process happened in your life—or the life of someone who has influenced you?

5. Scripture paints our purpose and calling in life as something that is set in motion long before we arrive on the scene. As Ephesians 2:10 says, "For we are God's workmanship, created in Christ Jesus to do good works, which God prepared in advance for us to do" (NIV).

How would you put that verse in your own words?

6. In this chapter, I quoted the apostle Paul's famous words about laying hold of the reason God laid hold of him. Listen to his words in their larger context:

Not that I have already obtained it, or have already become perfect, but I press on so that I may lay hold of that for which also I was laid hold of by Christ Jesus. Brethren, I do not regard myself as having laid hold of it yet; but one thing

I do: forgetting what lies behind and reaching forward to
what lies ahead, I press on toward the goal for the prize of
the upward call of God in Christ Jesus. (Phil. 3:12–14)

How does this verse encourage you concerning the *small
part* you are given to play in God's extraordinary drama?

7. Once again, beautiful and startling words are found in
Isaiah. Read the following passage prayerfully as words that
God would have you hear in some deeply personal way. How
do you sense him tapping you on the shoulder?

"I am the LORD, I have called You in righteousness,
I will also hold You by the hand and watch over You,
And I will appoint You as a covenant to the people,
As a light to the nations,
To open blind eyes,
To bring out prisoners from the dungeon,
And those who dwell in darkness from the prison.
"I am the LORD, that is My name;
I will not give My glory to another,
Nor My praise to graven images." (Isa. 42:6–8)

# Chapter 10

# JOURNEY WELL

1. When the apostle John was an old man on the island of Patmos, he described his journey with Christ as a mixture of "suffering and kingdom and patient endurance" (Rev. 1:9 NIV). In what ways are you seeing the truth of that in your own walk with God? What seems hopeful about his perspective?

2. Toward the end of Paul's life, he wrote letters to his son in the faith, Timothy. In one memorable line, Paul acknowledges that he sees himself as the chief of sinners, a living demonstration of Christ's patience and mercy (1 Tim. 1:15 KJV).

Yet Paul ends on a different note. The vision that motivated him is just two verses down. Read what Paul says in verse 17.

Now to the King eternal, immortal, invisible, the only God,
be honor and glory forever and ever. Amen.

Paul saw himself as the chief of sinners . . . but what focus dominated his life?

What would it mean for that same focus to dominate your own life?

3. What have you begun to sense that God is birthing in you—that, indeed, is a *becoming* that's taking place in your life?

Why is this worth the price you may pay?

4. Numerous scriptures make clear that the sacrifice of praise is, indeed, something that God highly values. Here are two clear examples of that truth:

"Offer to God a sacrifice of thanksgiving
And pay your vows to the Most High;
Call upon Me in the day of trouble;
I shall rescue you, and you will honor Me."
(Ps. 50:14–15)

Through Him then, let us continually offer up a sacrifice of praise to God, that is, the fruit of lips that give thanks to His name. (Heb. 13:15)

When does praise seem like a sacrifice in your life, and why do you think it honors God?

5. Describe three events or relationships that were challenging or difficult . . . but later, in retrospect, you found yourself strangely grateful that God brought that person or circumstance into your life.

How does the memory of that help with a present difficulty or one you think may be part of your future?

6. Moses begins Psalm 90 with these beautiful words.

Lord, you have been our dwelling place
    throughout all generations.
Before the mountains were born
    or you brought forth the earth and the world,
      from everlasting to everlasting you are God.(vv. 1–2 NIV)

When you think of your own journey with God through an uncertain life toward a certain future, what is deeply grounding about the truth expressed here?

7. One of the most beautiful benedictions in the New Testament occurs in the last verses of the book of Jude. As you read these verses, what is the picture that comes to mind? In what way do they serve to ground you in the present moment and encourage you in this awesome journey of following Jesus all your days?

Now to Him who is able to keep you from stumbling, and to make you stand in the presence of His glory blameless with great joy, to the only God our Savior, through Jesus Christ our Lord, be glory, majesty, dominion and authority, before all time and now and forever. Amen. (Jude 24–25)

*Let us hold unswervingly to the hope we profess,*
*for he who promised is faithful.*
(Heb. 10:23 NIV)

# NOTES

## CHAPTER 1: A DIFFERENT KIND OF WONDERFUL

1. J. B. Phillips, *Your God Is Too Small: A Guide for Believers and Skeptics Alike* (Carmichael, CA: Touchstone, 1997), n.p.
2. Ibid.
3. John Eldredge and Brent Curtis, *The Sacred Romance: Drawing Closer to the Heart of God* (Nashville: Thomas Nelson, 1997).

## CHAPTER 2: THE DANGER OF SETTLING

1. I've written more extensively about desire and longing in chapter 2 of *Strong Women, Soft Hearts* (Nashville: W, 2001), which you may find helpful on this subject.
2. Anne Sexton, "Courage," *The Complete Poems of Anne Sexton* (Boston: Houghton Mifflin, 1999), 425.

## CHAPTER 3: DISTURBING INTERRUPTIONS

1. Charles E. Moore, ed., *Provocations: The Spiritual Writings of Søren Kierkegaard* (Farmington, PA: Plough, 2002), excerpted from Howard V. Hone and Edna H. Hong, trans. and eds., *Søren Kierkegaard's Journals and Papers*, 7 vols. (Princeton, N.J.: Princeton University Press, 1967–1978), 194–95.
2. Derek Webb, "Introduction to I Repent," *The House Show,* Gospel Music USA, 2004.
3. C. S. Lewis, *The Problem of Pain* (New York: Macmillan, 1962), 43.
4. Psalms 56, 91, and 108.

## CHAPTER 4: OWNING YOUR STUFF

1. For further insight on Jungian psychology, see www.leannepayne.org/jung/index.php.
2. For further explanation, see Lawrence O. Richards, *Expository Dictionary of Bible Words* (Grand Rapids: Zondervan, 1991).

3. Sebastian Moore, *The Crucified Jesus Is No Stranger* (Mahwah, NJ: Paulist Press, 1977), 100.
4. Henri Nouwen, *The Return of the Prodigal Son* (New York: Doubleday, 1994), 40.
5. Ibid., 72.
6. Paula Rinehart, "Living As God's Beloved," *Discipleship Journal*, Issue 100, July/August 1997.
7. David Stewart, *Southern California Cold Waters* (Santa Ana, CA: n.p.).
8. This story comes from the annals of CoMission, a joint missions response to the invitation of the Russian Ministry of Education requesting help from Christians in the West as they sought to undo seventy years of atheism by teaching Christian morality and ethics in their public schools.
9. This practice of reading the Gospel accounts in present tense, as though one is there with Christ, has its ancient beginnings in the spiritual exercises of Ignatius, an early church father.

## CHAPTER 5: GROWING UP TOGETHER

1. Frederick Buechner, *Wishful Thinking: A Theological ABC* (New York: Harper & Row, 1973), 95.
2. Brennan Manning, *Abba's Child* (Colorado Springs: NavPress, 1994), 164.

## CHAPTER 6: COMING IN SECOND

1. I am indebted to Connally Gillam, friend and author of *The Revelations of a Single Woman: Loving the Life I Didn't Expect* (Carol Stream, IL: Saltriver, 2006), for this connection between *authority* and *author*.
2. Don Miller, *Blue Like Jazz* (Nashville: Thomas Nelson, 2003), 237.
3. Elisabeth Elliot, *Shadow of the Almighty: The Life and Testament of Jim Elliot* (San Francisco: HarperSanFrancisco, 1989), 160.
4. Ibid (emphasis in original).
5. C. S. Lewis, "Transposition," *The Weight of Glory* (New York: Macmillan, 1949), 55.
6. This story is from the annals of CoMission, 1990–1995.
7. Many Russians grew up during the years of Communism with their grandmothers, *babushkas*, as their only living connection to Christianity and the Bible.

## CHAPTER 7: THE EMPATHY OF JESUS

1. "The Power of the Cross Oh to See the Dawn," Keith Getty and Stuart Townsend, © 2005 Thankyou Music (kwy). All rights reserved. Used by permission.

2. Philip Yancey, *Soul Survivor* (New York: Doubleday, 2001), 214.

3. John Stott, *The Cross of Christ* (Downers Grove, IL: InterVarsity, 1986), 329 (as quoted in Stephen Seamands, *Wounds That Heal* (Downers Grove, IL: InterVarsity, 2003), 60.

4. "Imagine," Keith Getty and Kristyn Lennox, © Thankyou Music. All rights reserved. Used by permission.

5. "What a Friend We Have in Jesus," words: Joseph Scriven, 1855; and music: Charles Converse, 1868.

6. Dan Allender, author of *To Be Told*, refers to these distinctions as betrayal, abandonment, and humiliation—though I prefer these categories.

7. While I am unable to locate Updike's original comment, it is one that Frederick Buechner quoted in multiple contexts and is referenced by Philip Yancey, *Soul Survivor* (New York: Doubleday, 2001), 251.

8. My gratitude to Dr. Steven Breedlove, rector of All Saints Church, Chapel Hill, North Carolina, for this scriptural insight.

## CHAPTER 8: LOVING (DIFFICULT) PEOPLE

1. Eudora Welty, as quoted in *Blood Done Sign My Name*, Timothy B. Tyson (New York: Three Rivers, 2004), 325.

## CHAPTER 9: THE PLACE MEANT FOR YOU

1. Paula Rinehart, *Strong Women, Soft Hearts* (Nashville: W Publishing Group, 2001), 11.

2. Frederick Buechner, *Secrets in the Dark* (San Francisco: Harper Collins, 2006), 40.

3. Author's interview with Jesse Copeland in Raleigh, North Carolina, 2005.

4. Madeleine L'Engle, *The Ordering of Love* (Colorado Springs: Crosswicks, Ltd., 2005), 55. Used by permission of Waterbrook Press. All rights reserved.

5. Paula Rinehart, *Sex and the Soul of a Woman* (Grand Rapids:

Zondervan, 2004).

6. Charles E. Moore, ed., *Provocations: The Spiritual Writings of Søren Kierkegaard* (Farmington, PA: Plough, 2002), Ibid., 188.

7. "An Audience of One" is a wonderful phrase I first heard from Dallas Willard.

8. Flannery O'Connor, *Mystery and Manners: Occasional Prose* (New York: Farrar, Straus, and Giroux, 1969), n.p.

9. For a deeper understanding of these biblical concepts, see Col. 1:13; Isa. 49:6; Phil. 2:10; Ps. 50; 1 Cor. 3:21–23; Rev. 5:9–10.

## CHAPTER 10: JOURNEY WELL

1. Paul Delarouche, *The Execution of Lady Jane Grey*, The National Gallery of London, 1833.

## REFLECTION AND STUDY GUIDE

1. I heard Brennan Manning quote this benediction at a retreat many years ago.

2. Charles E. Moore, ed., *Provocations: The Spiritual Writings of Søren Kierkegaard* (Farmington, PA: Plough, 2002), Ibid., 125.

3. From a lecture by Francis Schaeffer in Ft. Worth, Texas, in 1978.

4. Richard Rohr, OEM and Paula D'Arcy, *A Spirituality for the Two Halves of Life* conference series (St. Anthony Messenger Press, 2004).

# ABOUT THE AUTHOR

*Paula Rinehart has touched women's lives through writing,* speaking, and personal ministry for more than twenty years. A professional counselor and author of *Strong Women, Soft Hearts; Sex and the Soul of a Woman;* and the bestseller, *Choices,* Paula speaks at women's conferences and women's retreats focused on personal growth and intimacy with Christ. She lives with her husband, Stacy, in Raleigh, North Carolina, where Stacy directs an international ministry, MentorLink, which develops leaders in countries where the church is growing rapidly. Stacy and Paula served for more than twenty years with the Navigators. They are parents of two grown children.

For more information on conferences and retreats, contact Paula at paularinehart@mentorlink.org or contact SpeakUp Speaker Services at speakupinc@aol.com. Paula's Web site is www.paularinehart.com.

# HAS THE DAY-TO-DAY BUSINESS OF LIVING ROBBED YOU OF PASSION AND VITALITY?

*P*aula Rinehart's *Strong Women, Soft Hearts* offers you hope and help. Paula writes as both a kindred spirit and a compassionate counselor to women feeling robbed of their passions and trapped by life's disappointing realities.

Using true stories, professional insights, and her own heartfelt wisdom—plus an assortment of practical exercises and questions in a newly expanded study guide—Paula helps you

* reconnect with long-lost dreams and refocus misplaced passion
* develop a vision for the *big picture* of your life
* discover when, how—and Whom—to trust

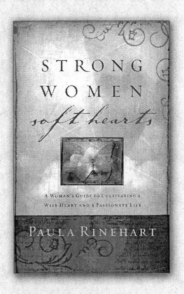

This book will help you listen and say *yes* to that call to become the strong, wise, loving, and and fufilled woman you were always meant to be.

THOMAS NELSON
*Since 1798*

ISBN: 978-0-8499-0997-9

CPSIA information can be obtained at www.ICGtesting.com
Printed in the USA
LVOW080507221012

303847LV00002B/2/P